IT'S OK TO BE GAY

D1355101

467 570 57 4

IT'S OK TO BE GAY

CELEBRITY COMING OUT STORIES

EDITED BY ALISON STOKES

"Being gay is maybe the 47th most interesting thing in my life. I want the whole process of 'coming out' to one day not be a big deal and if this book, and the work Diversity Role Models does in schools, contributes to that, then that's brilliant."

Sue Perkins

Acknowledgements

To all the celebrities, and their agents, who responded so promptly and positively to my Tweets and requests, and have given their time to be probed and quizzed, I thank you all.

To Suran Dickson, Paul Bradley, and Christopher Nicholls at Diversity Role Models. Thanks for putting me in touch with so many of your inspirational mentors. May you all continue to challenge homophobic behaviour and improve the lives of future generations.

Alison Stokes

Contents

Evan Davis   1

Val McDermid   9

Claire Harvey   15

Jane Czyzselska   25

Paul Burston   33

Lord Waheed Alli   41

Stella Duffy   47

Stifyn Parri   53

Rosie Wilby   63

Chris Needs   71

Alice Arnold   77

Shelley Silas   83

Phyllis Opoku-Gyimah   93

Nigel Owens   101

Charlie Condou   107

Jade Ellis   115

Edd Kimber   121

Sue Northover   131

Gareth Thomas   139

Robin Windsor   145

QBOY aka Marcos Brito   153

Diana King   159

Darren Scott   165

Sophie Ward   171

Foreword

When I first read the newspaper stories of Dominic Crouch, a 15-year-old who took his own life because there were rumours that he was gay, I couldn't get my head around it. Whether Dominic was gay or not no one will ever know, but the fact that a teenager could end his life due to this form of bullying just seemed too tragic for words. This sort of prejudice could and should be tackled to prevent this happening again.

Even as an openly gay teacher, working in some pretty tough schools in New Zealand and London, I had never encountered any problems. When my students found out I was gay, many had questions, but I answered them and they were fine. Some were kids who came from difficult backgrounds, who told me the homophobic beliefs of their parents, but they didn't have an issue with me and because we got on so well they defended me to others. I avoided any bullying at school as I was 19 when I had my first girlfriend, but I suspect I would have been OK at school. I had lots of friends, and was good at sport. But, I thought, it shouldn't have to be like that. There are many children who don't conform, many of them may not even be gay, but they are getting picked on for being different. These thoughts kept going round in my head until it got to the point where I had to do something.

At first I started by giving talks at a friend's school. I stood up in front of a class of young people I didn't know and asked 'What does the word gay mean?' The answer generally came back as 'naff, rubbish, ugly'. When I would reply 'That's a word I use to call myself – so are you saying I'm rubbish?' their general reaction was one of shock: 'No, no, we didn't mean you.' Most kids want to fit in and homophobic language is a fairly standard part of fitting in, particularly amongst teenage boys –until they meet someone who is gay and their perceptions are challenged and minds opened up to the potential damage they could cause. Two years ago I gave up my teaching job and registered Diversity Role Models as a charity. Our work is to send positive role models into primary schools, secondary schools and colleges to talk about their experiences and in doing so it gives young people the opportunity to think about how their attitudes and language can inadvertently affect real people.

This book puts into words the work of our role models. Several of the people in this book – Charlie Condou, Shelley Silas, and Claire Harvey – have all stood up in front of a class of young people to say they are gay. Once young people meet a role model the reaction is generally: 'You are just like me but you go out with someone who's the same sex as you – it's not actually a big deal.'

OK to be Gay gives young people – and adults too – the opportunity to read in private the stories of people from all walks of life, who just happen to be gay. Some, like rapper QBoy and radio presenter Chris Needs, have overcome bullying to make successes of their lives. UK Black Pride director Phyllis Opoku-Gyimah, Lord Alli, and Jamaican reggae star Diana King have experienced extreme cultural prejudice because of their sexuality, while *Dragons' Den* presenter Evan Davis conquered his own personal 'embarrassment' to find acceptance and happiness. I hope the people reading this book will find a connection with some of the contributors. Maybe they are David Bowie or Madonna fans, or maybe they support Arsenal. Maybe they are not even gay themselves, but having a common link and connection forms an understanding that helps eradicate homophobia.

Everyone should be able to be who they want to be. In schools I have met girls who are good at sport but are dropping out because they don't want to be called a lesbian and boys who hate sport with a passion but try hard just to fit in. It's not just about sexuality, it's all about being yourself and feeling able to be different. At Diversity Role Models we try to give children the confidence to be however they want to be. Robin Windsor's dancing talent has given him the opportunity to dance in front of millions of viewers every week as a professional on *Strictly Come Dancing*, while Edd Kimber's love of baking made him the first openly gay winner of The Great British Bake Off. The message we try to get across is: 'You will leave school, move on and find other people who love you for what you are.'

There is no doubt that the work we do and the stories told in this book will save lives. At the end of our sessions in schools we hand out evaluation forms. Some children write, 'I want to die because I'm being bullied.' Others will say, 'I think I'm like you but who do I go to?' It's good that we are able to show the teachers what's going on. It's 99% positive, however, with even the hardest, most homophobic young people saying, 'Gay people just seem normal, I shouldn't treat them any different.'

In recent years things have changed for the better for lesbian, gay, bisexual and transgender people. Equal marriage legislation does make a difference. There is something about the word that conjures up respect and when same-sex couples can say they are married, there is no longer a two-tier system of acceptance. Just a few years ago, before the Section 28 Clause of the Local Government Act was repealed in 2003, Diversity Role Models would not have been allowed to carry out workshops in school for fear of being seen as promoting homosexuality.

Through these stories, those people who are desperate and don't know to whom or where to turn, can have hope. Love is love, no matter what your culture or background and it is *OK to be Gay*.

Suran Dickson

CEO and Founder of Diversity Role Models

Evan Davis

Writer, Economist, Journalist, Presenter
Born: Worcestershire, 1962.

Best known as:
Presenter of the BBC reality business programme *Dragons'
Den* and BBC Radio 4's Today programme. He also presents
a weekly business discussion programme, The Bottom Line,
on Radio 4. Before joining the BBC in 1993, Evan was an
economist at the Institute for Fiscal Studies and at the London
Business School.

Evan Davis

What I think as being my coming out experience was Los Angeles. It was LA that made me gay. I first had a feeling that I might be gay just around puberty, but for the first couple of years I was tortured and tried hard to suppress any such desires.

I had struggled with my feelings all through my puberty. I grew up with my two older brothers in a fairly affluent family in Surrey. My childhood was happy and secure. My dad was an academic and my mum a social worker and psychoanalyst, so I had a science side from my father and a touchy-feely side from my mum. As a teenager I attended a state comprehensive school and was obsessed with Freddie Mercury and Queen. At the time he was remarkably inexplicit about his sexuality. It was fairly obvious to everyone, his sexuality was talked about and presumed but it wasn't spelled out. Whenever he was asked the question he would give ambiguous answers, so I wouldn't have called him an LGBT role model.

When I was 16, as I was doing my O levels, I spoke to someone about the feelings I was having. He told me that I should just enjoy them and shouldn't deny them any more. I realised that when you let yourself think about them, they're nice rather than horrible.

"I decided not to fight it any more and allowed myself to welcome and enjoy the gay feelings I was having. It was like the flicking of a switch – I was no longer tortured."

After puberty I assumed I was bisexual because I still had some feelings for women but by the time I went to Oxford University in 1981 I realised the feelings I had for women had been completely overtaken by those I had for men. Yet I still didn't feel comfortable identifying as gay. I hadn't told anyone at school. At university I wasn't out even though I was having boyfriends. It was all kept very quiet and I was quite embarrassed about it really. I think a few people did suspect but a lot didn't. After university I went to work in London, where I had a boyfriend, yet still we weren't out with our relationship. We would run off to the occasional gay bar we found, as in those days there weren't that many. We would keep it all very quiet as soon as we walked out of the door. I was always scared of being seen by someone I knew.

When I was 22, I went to the USA to study at Harvard University. My best friend there turned out to be gay. We had been best friends for three months before I knew. As a measure of how sensitive I was about being gay, I still didn't come out to him. I did subsequently tell him though!

After the first year at Harvard I had an internship at the utility company Southern California Edison in California. There I found a boyfriend of the same age, who was working for a record company and was about to study law at UCLA. In LA I didn't know anybody and everyone was so wilfully accepting of gayness in general, I was more comfortable with it. Gays were more visible, there seemed to be a comfort in crowds. Prior to that I had been self-isolating and made it unnecessarily difficult for myself. In LA I felt there was no need to worry – there are lots of gay people around and it was all very easy. It took LA to relax me: LA relaxes lots of people. I had never been further away from everyone I knew and I was able to carve a little life for myself for a few months. I became more comfortable with who I was, I met my boyfriend's parents and it provided a guide to what everything should and could be like. As a result I went back to Harvard the following term and was much more open and decided that I needed to tell my parents when I got back home to England.

I returned home from America in September and set myself a deadline to tell my family by Christmas. Lunchtime Christmas Day arrived and I still hadn't done the deed. I had already broken the news to one of my brothers during the drive to my parents' on Christmas Eve. I told him that I was going to tell Mum and Dad something very important about myself and asked him if he could guess what it was. Without much hesitation he said, "You're gay'. I told him that he was right and he suggested that I tell my parents in exactly the same way that I'd just told him. So I took his advice and as we were all sitting around after lunch on Christmas afternoon, I said to my parents that I had something important to tell them and asked if they could guess what it was. They didn't guess, but my brother, who I had told the previous day, intervened. Pretending he didn't already know, he said, "You're gay". It meant that I didn't actually have to say those words to my parents and made things a bit easier for me.

It was a bombshell, but it was late in the afternoon after an enjoyable lunch and they were fine about it. They were more shocked that they hadn't guessed. Looking back I think it would have been better if I'd told my parents when I first thought I might be gay. Leaving it until I was in my mid-twenties meant that my parents missed out on the opportunity to meet boyfriends and to be part of that aspect of my life, whereas if I had managed to tell them when I was 18 they could have been a part of it too.

I don't know what took me so long to tell my parents. I don't think I ever feared rejection as I had a loving family. I don't even think it was a fear of disappointing them. There was never any fear that my father would beat me or my mother would kick me out of the house, it was not an issue. It was down to a kind of shyness. Even in my pre-gay years I never talked to them about girlfriends, so I had this strange inhibition. I think it was just a sense of embarrassment. And to tell them you're gay, there's a sense that you're taking a different identity and you're not the same son they thought they had. You put something between you and you don't want to spoil things. As it happens you are putting something in between you when you don't tell them. It's right to tell them rather than have a gulf of secrecy.

Since coming out I am so much more relaxed and I do think it's nice for parents to share in your relationships. The most moving thing has been having a civil partnership with my French partner Guillaume in 2012 where we invited lots of people to the party afterwards and it was very touching to see people recognising and respecting our relationship.

"Acceptance is heart-warming. There's nothing like seeing how little people care about it and you cut yourself off from that acceptance if you don't tell them."

When I first joined the BBC I never really mentioned I was gay. But around the time I joined Newsnight in 1997 I decided I should definitely be publicly gay. It wasn't a courageous choice, it just felt to me that it was going to be slightly better to control the process by being up-front about it. Around this time *Gay Times* asked me if I wanted to do an interview and I jumped at the chance. It was quite pivotal for me career-wise. I did the interview before I was very famous and the fact that I got it out before anyone was interested meant there was no point at which it became a big deal or revelation and that was very helpful career-wise.

I've never been famous enough for any tabloid to be really interested in me, so I never had the public coming out moment. Potentially it could have been an issue when I started presenting *Dragons' Den* but I made sure it was out there before people were interested. Therefore I never really had that big moment where I had to sit down and say, "I'm gay and I've been hiding it for the past 15 years", or anything like that. Most people know and I'm very happy with that. I've never made a big issue of it. I don't think being gay has been a bonus on *Dragons' Den* but I do think in media circles being gay gives you one or two interesting points. Being interesting is important in the media and being gay is one component of potentially being interesting. I would go as far to say, and I fear it's sad, but the most interesting thing the press can write about me is that I'm gay and that's why the press do write about it quite often.

I don't want to be only defined by my sexuality and the danger is if you are a well-known gay journalist people associate you with one thing – the gayness. It's a more powerful signal to other people that you can just be a journalist who happens to be gay. I think it's useful there are people who show that life can be normal and you don't have to make gayness the centre of your life. It's a big part of your life but you don't want it to be the only part.

Since I first started presenting the Today programme in 2008 I have never found it difficult to be impartial on gay issues. Sometimes I would receive critical Tweets from people saying 'Why are you calling it gay marriage when it should be equal marriage?' because there's been a campaign to re-frame the debate by labelling it equal, rather than gay. I just replied by saying, 'Come on, you know it's really gay marriage and people won't know what we're talking about if we don't call it that – the need for clarity for our listeners matters more that your attempt to rephrase it.' I'm quite robust and strive to be impartial although some people might argue otherwise.

My advice to anyone who has yet to come out is – don't leave it too long. The longer you leave it the harder it gets. You end up having to break two bits of news; the first being that you're gay and the second that you have been lying or reticent. I also recommend being causal about it. If you're sensitive and make it an issue then you make other people more scared about it. I do think the trick of assuming they already know is good. You won't be able to get away with it with family and friends but when you start a new job, speak and act as though everybody already knows. So you don't necessarily tell people, you just say, "My boyfriend and I went to a movie on Saturday." People will be relaxed about it if you're relaxed about it. When you're too heavy about these things or too sensitive, you can create a vibe that makes others more self-conscious about it than they ought to really be. If you project an expectation that there may be some negativity you will create the negativity that you're afraid of. If you just expect that everyone will be cool with it, then it's much more likely that this will be the outcome.

Looking back to when I was younger, I can understand why I was so shy, but I wish I had been driven to come out earlier. I was more cautious than I needed to be and if I had done everything five or six years earlier with no perceptible change in outcome it would have meant I would have had six years of more relaxed and honest living. Life would have been easier.

Val McDermid

Author
Born Kirkcaldy, Scotland, 1955

Best known as:
Writer of the best-selling series of crime novels featuring
clinical psychologist Dr Tony Hill and DCI Carol Jordan, which
were adapted for TV as Wire in the Blood starring Robson
Green and Hermione Norris, and the Lindsay
Gordon Mysteries.

Val McDermid

As a child I had plenty of friends but I always felt like an outsider. I thought that was because I wanted to be a writer, but it was really more to do with being gay, I suspect.

I grew up in Kirkcaldy on the East Coast of Scotland, a small town famous for producing linoleum and for being the birthplace of the economist Adam Smith. It was at the heart of the Fife coalfield, and I spent a lot of my childhood with my grandparents, who lived nearby in a mining village. I was an only child so I had plenty of opportunity to lose myself in the worlds of imagination inside books.

My family lived opposite the central library, so I had access to a wide range of possibilities. As soon as I realised being a writer was a job, that was what I wanted to do. As a teenager I used to write songs and poems. I played guitar and sang in folk clubs, I played hockey, I was a champion debater and I spent a lot of time walking my dog and dreaming up stories in my head. I must have been about 10 when I had my first crush. It was Dusty Springfield. I cut out a picture of her from a magazine and stuck it on my wardrobe where I could see it from my bed.

"The realisation I was gay was more of a slow dawning through my teens rather than a moment of revelation. I think it had more to do with my gradual understanding that an alternative to being straight was possible"

There were no lesbians in Fife in the 1960s ... or at least, no visible ones. The first time I can remember being aware that homosexuals were real people was in my early teens.

There was a bit of a scandal when a local businessman left his wife to go off with another man. He was someone my father knew quite well, and I remember there was a definite shock wave in our community. But that seemed very far removed from my life.

At 17 I was accepted to read English at St Hilda's College, Oxford. There I first came out to my best friend as we were drinking coffee in her kitchen. She was completely blasé about it. It really seemed to make no difference to our friendship. The second friend I told had a totally different reaction. She was clearly very uncomfortable about it and it took years for us to get back on the same footing as before.

I was scared that by coming out I'd lose friends and that it would have a negative effect on my career. In fact almost all of my friends and family have been completely relaxed about it. I've been out for almost forty years now – which is a pretty wild thought for me – but of course, it's a constant process for all of us. Sometimes, to be honest, it feels more like a tedious chore than a source of fear or embarrassment.

Although I knew I wanted to write for a living, everyone told me that it was impossible and I should get a proper job. I knew I wasn't the sort of person who would be suited to a proper, nine to five, job so I became a journalist. For 14 years, I worked on national newspapers in Manchester and Glasgow. It was the 1980s and newsrooms were male-dominated. Some colleagues took my sexuality in their stride, some were uncomfortable with it, some took the piss and some just ignored it. I never experienced overt homophobia but I did work with one or two people who clearly had a problem with my sexuality. One news editor I worked for was a fanatically moralistic Catholic who went to mass every lunchtime. For about six months after he joined the paper, he simply ignored me. He wouldn't assign stories to me and when I generated my own story leads, sometimes he would pass them on to other reporters to follow up. Eventually I got so fed up that I engineered a meeting in the pub with the editor and pointed out they were paying me a helluva lot of money to do nothing. He saw my point. And my news editor clearly got a bollocking, because things changed almost immediately.

Since coming out I have had negative experiences but even in the negatives there have been positive moments. Once my girlfriend and I took my mum on holiday to the Highlands. In Oban, the B&B we were sent to by the tourist board refused to give me and my girlfriend a room with a double bed. My mum read the riot act to the owner then insisted on going back to the tourist office to complain about the offensive treatment we'd received.

"My mum's reaction turned what could have been a (moment of) humiliation into a moment of pride."

Being open about my sexuality has opened up story possibilities that I might otherwise have shied away from. I think a life in the closet is a life half-lived and that's a terrible restriction for a writer. Always to be looking over your shoulder and worrying if you're revealing too much is self-censorship of the worst kind. And of course, it's given me access to all sorts of experiences and environments that I would otherwise have missed out on. Since everything is material, that has to be a help!

In 1984 I started writing *Report For Murder*, the first in the series of Lindsay Gordon books which features a lesbian freelance journalist as the central character. I was lucky enough to start my career at a time when there were feminist presses who were eager to publish lesbian fiction. So in my head there was no reason why Lindsay couldn't be a lesbian. Most writers start off by writing close to their own lives in one way or another – either literally or emotionally or psychologically – so I gave Lindsay a lot of the superficial elements of my life – nationality, sexuality, politics, occupation – because I understood how to write about those things. But she's a very different personality from me, I should stress!

Those early books taught me a huge amount about my craft. I planned to write a trilogy, but it ended up as six books over a period of sixteen years. Like all writers, I'm on a journey of constant development and challenge so I don't know if I'll ever go back to her; I can only write the books that shout loudest in my head and she's not been doing much shouting lately.

My advice to young people struggling to come to terms with their sexuality is to decide who you can trust and make that person your confidant. The fears and doubts that loom huge in our imagination are cut down to size when we share them with somebody who doesn't condemn us, somebody who loves and cares for us regardless of who we want to have relationships with.

Claire Harvey

Paralympian
Born: Medway, 1972

Best known as:
Team captain for GB women's sitting volleyball team and only
openly lesbian athlete of the Paralympic Games 2012.

Claire works as Diversity & Inclusion Co-ordinator at the
Financial Services Authority.

Claire Harvey

As a child I was very sporty, I enjoyed running and football and rugby, but I didn't fit in with the other sporty girls at school who played netball. I couldn't grasp the concept of netball, for me holding the ball and standing still was just bizarre. I had little interest in make-up and clothes, clothes for me were just things to put on to enable me to go and climb trees. I was an absolute tomboy and got on with the boys better than the girls. Anything that could be climbed or covered in mud – I was there. The other kids called me 'Weirdo' because my surname at the time was Weir.

"I would watch Wimbledon and was fascinated by the female tennis players. As I grew older I realised it was sexual attraction but at the time it was just a reaction."

I was besotted with the American player Mary Jo Fernandez. At the time I couldn't tell if she was a good tennis player or not, she obviously was as she was made it to the semi-finals in 1991 when she was beaten by Steffi Graf, but I was fascinated by her grace and her physique. Around the same time I also had a massive crush on my PE teacher. PE was my favourite lesson and I was always well behaved and would do anything to please her. If ever I saw her car outside school I was beside myself with excitement.

When I hit puberty I realised it was girls I found attractive, not boys, and struggled with my sexuality. I decided to join my local rugby team as that's where it seemed there might be a group of women who were gay and I might fit in. I joined Medway women's rugby club where I was the youngest player in the team. In one way it was hugely beneficial as it gave me exposure to a community I didn't understand. But it was the 1980s, and a lot of the women playing the game were ex-forces and were quite butch and it made me question if I was gay or not because I didn't find butch women attractive. I never had any feminine female role models, so was still quite confused.

I first came out to one of my friends in the team, who was older. I was 14 at the time and had a massive crush on her sister, who was 21. It was the end of season dinner and I had written her sister a poem. I asked my friend if her sister had a girlfriend or if I could give her a poem. My friend thought it was quite funny and entertained me, telling me her sister would be flattered. After that when I first started telling people I was gay they were like 'No shit, Sherlock!' It was such a big deal to me and I couldn't understand why it wasn't such a big deal to the others, who were older and more mature.

At the age of 16 I started playing premiership rugby which meant going on tour. It was during one of those tours to Amsterdam that I lost my virginity to another player. Out on tour the older women on the team protected me: I wasn't allowed to drink and they made sure I didn't. Looking back I must have been the most horrendous player. I was at that age, at the beginning of sexual awareness, where I was just a ball of teenage emotion. I was 16 and really precocious. I thought I knew better than anyone. Quite frankly I don't know how the rest of the team didn't kill me. I would flirt with anyone and everyone. It was almost mandatory for me to find someone to chase while on tour, I simply couldn't go on tour and just play rugby. I think it's common at that age, where copping off is such a big deal. I felt like I was beginning to find my identity and being in a relationship was my way of feeling valued and validated.

Telling my family I was a lesbian was quite awkward. I was 16 and in a relationship with a girl who was six years older and lived in Essex. Every weekend I would go on the train and spend the weekend with her, telling my mum I was going to stay with rugby friends. Some weekends she would drive down to Medway and pick me up. One weekend I came home and I was sitting in the living room while my mum was doing the ironing. She asked where I'd been.

'I've been out with Helen. We've been talking about rugby,' I secretively replied.

'Do you think I'm stupid?' she snapped. Then went on to say something like 'Does this girl have golden tits?' She was just being protective, but I didn't know how to react. I went on the defensive shouting, 'How dare you! You must have been reading my mail.'

After that there was silence for a long time, followed by lots of crying. My parents were less concerned by the fact she was a woman and more concerned that she was six years older than me.

On reflection I was pretty much her lap-dog, but wasn't in a position to see it any differently. She would dump me and I would go crawling back. All the people around me could see it and would say things like, 'You can do better'. But I was 16 and besotted.

I put on a very good defence that I didn't care what anyone else thought, but when I look back to how I behaved it was really destructive as deep down I did care what people thought but I couldn't voice those feelings. I would ram my sexuality down people's throats, making a big deal about it. One time we were having a sex education lesson in school and I walked out of the class and made a big scene about how they were talking about heterosexual sex and that wasn't inclusive and that wasn't my life. 'Actually I've had sex lots of times and it happens to be with a woman. So what do you think about that?' I said to the teacher. It was wholly the wrong way to go about it but I was so desperate to get someone to acknowledge my sexuality that I tried to bring it up at every opportunity and that made it inappropriate. It was my way of trying to get people to talk about it.

I'm sure from the outset I was determined I was going to be the different one but with hindsight I hated the fact that people couldn't accept who I was. Now I can see how I perpetuated some of that because I made it such a big deal all the time. The sad part is that in my desperation for acceptance I didn't see the people who really did care.

"I had some really good friends who tried to take me under their wing but I couldn't deal with it because I couldn't accept who I was as I lacked self-esteem."

My behaviour was fuelled by the fact that I believed no one would find me attractive. Yet I have since discovered from friends that there were lots of people who found me attractive. I was young, nubile, cocky and a very good rugby player but I never saw beyond my own desperation.

The turning point came when I went to university. Initially I had no intention of going to university. Even though my teachers told me I was intelligent and had the ability to do well, I was determined not to. I had dropped out of school before sitting my A Levels and moved into a flat with my girlfriend and got a job as a lifeguard. Shortly after that I broke the relationship off. My PE teacher, who was the only one I would listen to, talked me into going back and sitting my exams. I passed with better results than I had expected and decided I wanted to get as far away from Medway as I could. So when I was offered a place studying psychology in Liverpool, I packed my car and left. It was the best thing that could have happened to me. I had built up a reputation in our small community and found it difficult to change people's opinions of me. Moving to Liverpool I was able to reinvent myself, I also met a broader group of gay women, who looked different. Some were sporty, some weren't. I met many more women who made me realise that I could have long hair and be quite girlie and that was OK. As a teenager I shaved my hair and wore dungarees, trying to identify with what I thought a lesbian should look like. Being 5ft 5in tall and built like a piece of wet string, that look didn't work for me. At university I realised I could be who I was and people would actually like me for being just me. I grew my hair, felt more comfortable about how I looked and went with the flow. My hormones had calmed down and I wasn't so manic around women. Growing up and being surrounded by different role models things started to slot into place.

"When I joined the GB Sitting Volleyball team in 2009 I had to make a conscious decision whether to come out to my team mates or not."

A year before I had had an accident which left me paralysed in one leg and needing crutches and a wheelchair. I still wanted to be play sport and decided to go along to a British Paralympic Association talent day, where I tried out different sports and I found I had a talent for sitting volleyball. A couple of months later the BPA brought five of us, who it thought had potential, together to form a training team for London 2012. It was the first time that sitting volleyball was to be included in the Paralympics. At that point we were all strangers and everyone was asking questions about one another. It was interesting as it was the first time in a very long time I had to make such a decision whether to come out and it took me back to being a teenager.

When you are older and have been in a relationship for a certain length of time you have a very solid social circle of friends. I had been with my partner Clare for many years, we had two children, and our sexuality was almost irrelevant. But at the point of meeting my team – other members would ask what my husband did and I took the decision I was going to say something. I had learnt from previous experience the less you say the harder it becomes. 'They either want me for who I am or they don't. If they don't want me I'll leave,' I thought.

At first there were a couple of members of the team who were uncomfortable and were nervous about sharing a room with me, but that was out of ignorance rather than anything else as they had seen so many lesbians portrayed as predators in the media, therefore they thought all gay women were like that. Some members of the team were more inclusive and were very good in telling the others about times they had shared with lesbians in complete safety. With the women who were unsure I gave them time and a safe environment to talk about their concerns and ask questions and they were able to break down all those assumptions they had formed. There were some younger girls in the team would use the words 'it's so gay'. There was one 16-year-old girl who used the phrase so much it was part of her vocabulary until one day I said to her 'I actually find that quite offensive.' She hadn't associated the word 'gay' with me but she soon stopped using it in such a way.

I found it bizarre being hailed the only out lesbian in the 2012 Paralympics. I was being interviewed and the interviewer asked about my Paralympic journey. I explained that my partner had encouraged me to go to the open day. They asked my partner's name and I replied 'Clare'. I had no understanding of the interest that would cause. Clare and I had been together for a long time, so I didn't even think about the answer. I was just surprised that I was the only one. I'm sure I'm not the only one but if others haven't come out it's difficult to go back and do it. There's also the issue of sponsorship and people fear what companies might do, although I don't actually think they care. But if your sport is reliant on sponsorship you don't want to rock the boat – so you don't ask. The sitting volleyball team was not sponsored so in the bigger scheme of things I had nothing to lose.

On a personal level coming out enabled me to give everything to my sport. I could be exactly who I was and not have to worry about hiding things – as I'm a rubbish liar.

It helped me to focus all my attention on the games. There is no way I would have got to the Paralympics if I had to keep some of myself back. I'm not intelligent enough to do that; I would have tripped myself up a million times. All the time I spent away from home and not being able to call my partner and not having her come to pick me up from the airport or even acknowledge her in that journey would have been horrendous and the team would not have respected me.

> **"Being out has also helped others. I'm not a superstar, I'm not even a gold medal-winning Paralympian, but I have had letters from young people who are encouraged by my openness to be themselves."**

I've been involved in drawing up the government's charter to create accreditation for clubs so that young people know that if clubs have a charter mark it's a safe place for them. Being out not only helped me to get where I am in the games but to create a legacy. I hope I play a small part in making life easier for other LGBT people to get involved in sport and to make it a more inclusive place. I don't think I'm remarkable but I'm more vocal than some people and if by speaking out I can makes someone's life better, I feel very humble to do that. I am also a patron of Diversity Role Models and I believe educating young people will help the next generation deal better with coming out than I did.

Jane Czyzselska

Journalist
Born: London, 1969

Best-known as:
Editor of *DIVA*,
best-selling magazine
for lesbian and bi
women

Jane Czyzselska

When I was 14 I remember thinking 'Oh God, I really hope I'm not a lesbian.' It's awful to think I had such negative thoughts but I went to a school in London where there was a distinct atmosphere of lesbophobia. The only time the word lesbian was ever used was in name-calling like 'lezzie' or 'lesbi-friends.' Deep down I knew I probably was a lesbian.

A year earlier I'd had an experience with a friend which at the time I thought little of. It was only when I hit puberty and became more sexually aware that I realised we'd had a 'lesbian' experience and I had a sense of who and what I might be. The incident was never mentioned again. But reflecting back, with no lesbian role models or visibility, I understand why I hoped I wasn't gay, living in such a lesbo- and homophobic culture.

"During my school years I had crushes on teachers, but didn't perceive it in a sexual way. I was slightly bashful around my teachers and older girls at school but I didn't think of it as lesbian – I just felt it was normal – other girls had crushes too, after all."

My earliest crush was on a girl called Emma. She was a few years older than me and I followed her everywhere. When she left school she gave me a present – a necklace. With that gift I thought I would die happy. I also had a really bad crush on my biology teacher. As well as taking notes in biology lessons, I would write notes in my teenage diary about what she was wearing and how she smiled at me. I had it bad. Around the same time, though, I also had a crush on a boy who looked like Robert Smith from The Cure. In my teens I had a boyfriend simply because all the girls did. It was a rite of passage and measure of how cool you were because boys were interested in you. I wasn't interested in "Robert" sexually, though. I had cravings for women but didn't act on those feelings until I moved away from home to university and joined the Lesbian and Gay Society. There I met my first girlfriend and gradually I came out to my housemates, who accepted me, in the main.

When I came out to one of my closest straight female friends though, she didn't react well at all. I thought we were good friends but she was really uncomfortable when I told her I thought I might be a lesbian. In those days you didn't say you were gay to be fashionable and I felt I was ostracised by her.

My parents were quite liberal and open-minded in many ways, but when I came out to them they had a 'wobbly' moment. They had two gay male friends, who were a couple and whom I always considered to be my 'gay dads' but when I told them about me they were concerned at how open I was going to be about my sexuality. At the time I was still in university and writing for a gay publication. I decided to take a new surname 'Czyzselska' – a name that was based on the last name of one of my gay dads, so as not to pour oil on troubled waters, and the name stuck.

"The most positive thing about being a lesbian is being free of a lot of society's expectations. In our patriarchal society women are still valued less than men and not having to buy into all that because I'm a lesbian is great."

I like the fact that I haven't followed the traditional heterosexual path in life. There's something liberating about not having to fit wholesale into mainstream expectations.

That said, I believe marriage should be open to everyone from the standpoint of basic equality. I'm thrilled that we will be free to marry from 2014.

I have always worked in the media. When I left university I worked at the BBC and as a freelance journalist for the broadsheet national newspapers. When I first started writing it was difficult to get gay stories placed in mainstream newspapers because our lives were considered irrelevant. I once pitched a story to *The Independent* about an Iranian lesbian who was facing deportation under the then Home Secretary Jack Straw. She was clearly being sent back to her death. She would face 100 lashes if she was found to be a lesbian, which would be difficult to hide.

My story was about how unjust it was – the issue of sending gay people back to their death. It took a long time to convince the news editor it was a relevant social injustice story. I said, 'Imagine if you were the only straight person in a gay world and you had to hide for fear of the death penalty.' He eventually got it and ran the story.

When *Diva* magazine was launched some 19 years ago, I started contributing stories. I took over as editor nine years ago and in February 2013 we celebrated our 200th issue. Being editor of *Diva* is a huge privilege and responsibility. It's really challenging to meet the needs of the various communities all the time. There are different communities of lesbians and bisexuals just as there are different communities of heterosexuals but there are many different magazines catering to different niches – *Diva* has to be all things to all queer women.

As editor I think it's important for the magazine to feature positive images of what lesbians are and can be as well as reporting on the more challenging aspects of our lives – we try to feature a broad age range of women who face similar yet unique experiences. We interview artists, activists, writers, film makers, musicians, lesbians serving in the forces and lesbian parents as well as including reader stories to try and present as many different facets of lesbian and bisexual life as possible. We hope we inspire our readers and create thought-provoking features and interviews.

There is a much greater range of lesbian identities in the public awareness today and that can only be a good thing although sometimes old stereotypes linger. I remember a couple of years ago I had an email from a reader saying 'Jane is looking more and more heterosexual in her photographs'. I don't know why she thought that but she did. At the time my photograph showed me wearing a denim shirt with shoulder-length curly blonde hair. I've done every lesbian look going. Before that it was dinner jacket, white T-shirt and dark curly hair; on another occasion it was checked shirt and straight hair. I've exhausted all the lesbian looks over the years, yet I didn't conform to that reader's particular idea of the stereotype lesbian. That said, our readers are also subject to stereotyped views of how lesbians should look and behave. We've recently launched our Everyday Lesbophobia campaign – based on the Everyday Sexism project – to highlight and document just how much prejudice still exists towards lesbians. Comments like "you're too pretty to be a lesbian," "which one's the man?" or "can I join in?" or lesbians being shouted at in the street in an attempt to shame them are reactions that our readers experience to their sexuality on a disappointingly frequent basis.

I often get letters from people of all ages thanking *Diva* for helping them to accept it's OK to be gay. Perhaps over time, as more people attend the marriages of their gay family members and friends this prejudice will wane but I suspect it will take a few more generations for the collective shame many feel about being gay or lesbian to disappear, if it ever will. Despite this it's important to remember that we're in a far stronger position today in the UK than we've ever been and we shouldn't forget that. Compared to many of our gay brothers and sisters elsewhere in the world we are at least no longer outlaws. We must use this relative freedom to continue to highlight the injustice they and others face.

Share your stories of Everyday Lesbophobia at www.everydaylesbo.com, @EverydayLesboph and like our page on Facebook.

Paul Burston

Journalist, Writer, Political Activist
Born: York, 1965

Best known as:
'The UK's Armistead Maupin' with his books *Shameless*, *The Gay Divorcee*, *Lovers and Losers* and *Star People*. Stonewall Award-winning editor of the LGBT section of *Time Out London* magazine. Also host of London's LGBT literary salon Polari at the Southbank Centre

Paul Burston

I was 18 when I left home and moved to university in London. For me, going to university wasn't simply about getting an education – it was about being gay. It was a chance to be somewhere else, somewhere where I could finally be myself. And to me, London represented that. But it would be another five months before I actually came out.

I came to London in September 1984. Frankie Goes to Hollywood and Bronski Beat were in the charts that year, and London had this image as a place where people ran away to be gay. Growing up in Bridgend, a small town in south Wales, I had no role models. I remember being at home with my stepdad one night, while my mum was working night shifts as a nurse, and the television film The Naked Civil Servant was on TV. Now I watch it and can appreciate what an incredible man Quentin Crisp was, but as a 10-year old boy, who was coming to terms with feeling different, to see this highly effeminate character was pretty terrifying. At that time there were people like John Inman and Larry Grayson on TV but they were portrayed as camp clowns. There were no gay characters in soap opera or dramas like *Queer as Folk* that portrayed gay men as real people.

From the age of 14, I gravitated towards David Bowie because he was the only person I knew of who made homosexuality seem cool, something to aspire to, rather than something shameful and dirty and secretive. My bedroom wall was covered in Bowie posters.

By the time I got to the sixth form my obsession with Bowie had grown in a big way. My friends in the sixth form were all heterosexual, but we all wore make-up and earrings and looked pretty outrageous – it was the Eighties after all. I had a girlfriend as all my friends did. I shaved my eyebrows off and dyed my hair pink. But the more bizarre I looked, the more girls seemed to like me. I looked completely freaky yet I was denying I was gay. I didn't think it was possible to be gay in Bridgend at that time – it was pretty hostile. It was years later that I found out there were lots of things going on in my school that I had no knowledge of – often the last people I would have thought of.

In London I studied English, film and drama and for the first couple of months I didn't tell anyone I thought I might be gay. I would spend my evenings alone in the cinema. Then one night I spotted two lads in the front row, they looked like they might be a couple. So when the film ended I followed them. I tracked them all around the West End of London for half an hour until they arrived at Heaven.

"I had heard about Heaven, it was the most famous gay club in the world. Frankie Goes to Hollywood had filmed a video there. The boys went into the club but I waited outside. For two hours I chain-smoked trying to pluck up the courage to go in."

I was terrified because all the men going in looked like lumberjacks, they were macho and wore checked shirts and big moustaches, and there I stood, a pink-haired freak. I went home. The following week I went back to Heaven and had the guts to go in.

It was like nothing I had seen before – a place where men were dancing with men and being themselves. In Heaven I had my first sexual experience. I met someone and went home with him and from that moment I completely understood that this is who I am.

Once I came out to my friends in college, I came out in a really big way. I became very outspoken and political, which didn't go down so well with some of the other students. They thought I was drawing too much attention. I wanted to start a Lesbian and Gay Society, but in a Catholic college that didn't go down too well with the authorities. As a teenager I had always been political, joining CND ban the bomb marches. I had overcome my fear of myself and I became angry at the injustice of everything. It was the early 1980s and there was a lot to be angry about. I could have been put in prison for going out and acting on my desire as it was still illegal for men under the age of 21 to be actively homosexual. I felt it was important to make a statement, but not all of my friends felt the same way. Even though some of my friends were gay, and my closest female friend later turned out to be a lesbian, at that time they were not keen on the attention I attracted.

Initially I decided to hide my sexuality from my parents. It was 1985, the media was full of scaremongering stories about AIDS – the 'gay disease' and I was concerned they would worry about me so I didn't tell them the finer details of my life in London.

During one of the Easter holidays while I was at home, I lied to my parents. I told them I was going back to London early to stay with a friend from college. Actually I had met a guy and was going to stay with him. However, when I got to his house I discovered he had a long-term partner. It was my first gay heartbreak. I couldn't go back home as I would have had to explain to my parents. So I had no choice but to stay at this guy's house. I got through the week by reading Oscar Wilde's *De Profundis* and thinking. I decided it was time to come out to my parents.

I sat down and drafted a letter which was modelled on Michael Tolliver's Letter to Mama from my favourite author

Armistead Maupin's *Tales of the City*. I posted the letter and waited. A week passed and no one called which was odd as we spoke every week without fail. When she didn't ring I worried and called her. My stepdad, who is a builder, answered the phone. 'Can I talk to Mum?" I asked. 'She's not ready to talk to you yet, she's still dealing with it,' he replied. 'You seem all right with it,' I ventured, slightly shocked as up until that point I had thought of my stepdad as an old-school, macho builder type. 'I know loads of gay people in the building trade,' he confessed, which was a bit of an eye-opener. He then went on to tell me about a transgender prostitute he knew, which really freaked me out.

A week later I spoke to my mum and it was all fine. Like most parents, she was concerned for my safety. 'I worry you might get attacked out on your own in London,' she admitted. I reassured her that it was fine and I would be careful. Homophobia is still an issue.

"Gay people still can't walk down the street with their partner and not get a reaction, but back in the mid-1980s there was more fear of the unknown. In my mother's mind if I was going to be gay I was going to get beaten to death."

Coming out to my family felt like a weight had been lifted off my shoulders. No one can live a healthy life in the closet. It's a horrible way to live. In my job as a journalist I often interview actors and professionals, who I know or suspect to be secretly gay, yet they are afraid they'll lose their fanbase if they come out. It's a terrible way to live your life. It's not who you love that defines who you are and to be forced to deny that part of yourself does so much harm to your psychological well-being. For many, the biggest thing about coming out is the anxiety of rejection, but that goes away quickly. Coming out is not an event, it's an on-going process – you come out every day of your life. For 25 years I have been a gay activist, writer and journalist. I worked for the London gay police monitoring project GALOP and was an activist with the AIDS advocacy group ACT-UP London, yet I still have situations where I think, 'Do I disclose this or not?' I travel around the UK and abroad and there are some places where I don't feel as safe as I would if I were walking around Soho and at those times I have to check myself and wonder how much to reveal. I have been queer-bashed several times. I get verbal abuse quite regularly because I look identifiably gay. A gay man was beaten to death in front of tourists in Trafalgar Square in 2009 so it still happens and you have to be on your guard. I have been attacked and hurt. But I found the answer by finding the most fierce lesbian kick-boxer and asking her to teach me self-defence. The next time a bloke tried to attack me, as I was walking home, I gave him the surprise of his life when I fought back.

Things are definitely getting easier for gay people these days. Legislative changes like the Civil Partnership Act, which came into being in 2005 giving same-sex couples the same rights and responsibilities of marriage and more recently the Marriage (Same Sex Couples Bill) which the government approved in February 2013 and gives gay couples the equality to get married, make a difference. The minute the law says gay people should have the same rights as straight people, it sends out a positive message.

The biggest fear when you're young is the belief that you are the only one in the world. Young people today don't have the same fear that my generation had. It's a different world. There are so many online social networks. They can go on Twitter and Facebook and find other people, they might be in the same street or another country but they will find them. Social networking has had a profound effect on how young people can come out. And once they come out there's a different expectation as to what their lives can be. There is still pressure but a lot less. I came out in a world where it was illegal to be gay until you were 21, there was the Section 28 clause of the Local Government Act, which banned schools from promoting homosexuality. So young people couldn't be openly gay in schools and, if you were a gay teacher, you had no protection in your job. Despite all these changes homophobia still hasn't gone away. The battle for hearts and minds isn't won yet. It will take another 15 or 20 years before things will change to a point where every LGBT person feels totally safe but it's a lot better than it used to be.

Lord Waheed Alli

Labour peer and entrepreneur
Born: London, 1965

Best known as:
The youngest and first openly gay peer in the House of Lords
and media mogul behind shows such as *The Word*, *The
Big Breakfast*, *Survivor* and the children's show *Octonauts*.
Played a key role in lowering the age of consent for gay sex
from 18 to 16 and the repeal of Section 28, which banned the
promotion of homosexuality by local authorities. Helped to
spearhead the gay marriage debate in the House of Lords.

Lord Waheed Alli

On 13 April 1999 the House of Lords heard a speech quite unlike any other it had heard before. At 10.29pm, after more than six hours of debate, the youngest member of Britain's Upper House stood up and declared:

"I am openly gay. I am 34. I was gay when I was 24, when I was 21, when I was 18, and even when I was 16. I have never been confused about my sexuality. I have [only ever] been confused about the way I am treated as a result of it."

It may seem less extraordinary now but then Lord Alli of Norbury was the first peer to have ever spoken openly about being gay in the House of Lords. In fact, he was the first member of Britain's upper house to admit to being gay at all.

Over the next few minutes, he quietly explained why legislation for an equal age of consent was not just a moral right but also a moral imperative. He described how he had been forced to keep his relationships secret from his employers, friends and even his family and been labelled as 'sick', 'abnormal' and 'unnatural' simply for being gay. He concluded: 'In tonight's vote I should like your Lordships to speak out for me and millions like me, not because you approve or disapprove, but because if you do not protect me you protect no one.'

In the intervening 14 years Parliament has voted not only for an equal age of consent (1999), but also for the right for gay couples to adopt (2005), to openly serve in the military (2000), for the repeal of section 28 (2003) for civil

43

partnerships (2005) and a host of other anti-discriminatory legislation.

As Alli puts it: 'If you told me when I went into the House of Lords 14 years ago that there would be a black President of the United States and that a Conservative Prime Minister would put forward legislation for gay marriage, I just wouldn't have believed it. Things have just changed so much. If you're black, if you're a woman, if you're disabled, if you're gay, there is no time in history, no place on earth that it would have been better to have been in than 1997 onwards.

'In 1999 when I was involved in the first piece of gay equality legislation I was called "'sinful", "disgraceful" and "dirty". And that was in a debate in the House of Lords – it was awful. I'd only been there a few months. When the whip came back and reported that we'd lost by a huge number, I felt physically sick.

'I thought, I hate this place and I don't want to be here. This is just the most awful place. Why on earth do I want to be here? But then Margaret Jay, who was Leader of the House of Lords, stood up and walked to the despatch box and said, "My Lords, I am instructed by my Right Honourable Friend the Prime Minister to inform this House that he will for only the second time this century use the Parliament Act to ensure safe passage of this Bill on to the Statute Book." In that one moment I thought, Tony Blair – you did what Bill Clinton didn't do. You didn't walk away from this. You absolutely took it through.

Every single year afterwards the Lords have put through a piece of equality legislation – and never lost another vote. The opponents of gay marriage are divided into two groups: those who have deeply held religious views and a second group who oppose now but will probably repent later.

They were the type of people who voted against the equalisation of consent and regretted it. They are the people who voted against civil partnerships and regretted it. And I'll believe those who voted against gay marriage will regret it in five years' time.

I have nothing but respect for David Cameron for bringing forward the legislation against such opposition. I think he just believes in it. It's a personal commitment. It's in his DNA.

'I want to win the ground and keep it. I never want to go back to where we were.'

Adapted from an interview by Oliver Wright, first published in *the Independent* on Sunday, June 2 2013.

Three days after the interview, after two days of debate the House of Lords voted two to one in favour of the Marriage (Same Sex Couples) Bill. On July 17 2013 the bill became law enabling gay couples in England and Wales to get married in both civil and religious ceremonies.

Reproduced with permission.

Same-Sex Marriage ebook is published by *The Independent* and collects reports published in *The Independent* over more than two decades, retracing the long, hard journey to change.

Stella Duffy

Writer and theatre director
Born: London, 1963

Best known as:
Author of thirteen novels including *The Purple Shroud*, *The Room of Lost Things* and *State of Happiness*. Wife of Shelley Silas.

Stella Duffy

I was in my mid-late teens when I realised I might be gay. It was pretty simple – I fancied women and girls at school. At the time I didn't know what lesbians were and, as far as I knew, I had never met any, so I didn't know if that was normal or not, but I assumed it wasn't.

I grew up in a really small timber town, Tokoroa in New Zealand, where almost three quarters of the people were either Maori or Polynesian, so I was slightly 'outside' already anyway. My father was originally from New Zealand and he and my mother left our home on a south London council estate and emigrated there when I was five. Leaving Britain so young, I benefitted from a much better education than I would have had if we stayed in south London.

In Tokoroa in the late 1960s and early 1970s there were no lesbian role models on TV, in the movies, in books or even in my life. The town had only one cinema, which showed films at the weekend, so I had a very limited access to any role models. In retrospect it felt like a very closed life but at the time I didn't know any different.

"At school there were girls I had a deep friendship with but thought nothing of it. I also fancied boys, so having those types of feelings didn't come as a huge shock. It was only when I got older I realised what the attraction was."

During my time at university I went to see the Topp Twins in concert. It was the early eighties and there on stage were two identical twins, Lynda and Jools, who were both gay and successful and I thought, "OK, people can do this."

You have to understand that up until that time it wasn't that I thought it was terrible to be gay, I simply didn't know it was possible. I had watched the film *The Killing of Sister George* and thought that if you were gay you wanted to kill yourself – because that was the only portrayal of lesbians around. It seemed that all the other gay women I met around this time wanted to be gay because they didn't like men, and I didn't fit in. That was not me. Although I had, and still do have, strong feminist politics, I didn't fit into the stereotypes of the time.

The turning point for me came when I joined the gay society at university. There I met gay women who were not only out but wore great 1950s frocks which they bought from the 'op shops' (charity shops).

"It might sound funny now, but in 1981 it was a huge deal; it was so unusual for women who wore their hair long and wore groovy frocks to identify as a lesbian."

It was then that I realised I was gay and that what I was feeling was something more than just being in love with my best friend at school.

When I told my parents I was gay, they were both completely fine. At the time political campaigners in New Zealand were trying to lower the age of consent for gay sex from 18 to 16 to create parity with heterosexuals. So homosexuality was part of the political agenda. My mum's response was 'You'll probably find a lot more companionship with a woman than a man.' She also told me that she had seen a lot of lesbianism when she was in the army during WWII. When I told my dad he said, 'It doesn't change my relationship with you.' I was amazed and delighted that he was so accepting. Both my parents came from white working class families and I was the first person in our family to go to university, they were political but not especially 'liberal', so I hadn't really expected them to react so well.

I think that part of the reason for their positive reaction was because I didn't present it like it was going to be a problem. If you tell your parents 'Sit down, I've got something to tell you,' that sounds like someone has died. We're buying into society's belief that it is a problem. I never did, I just dropped it into the conversation and it was completely fine.

For me being gay has never been a big deal or the most interesting thing about me. I still don't think it is, but the world does. I was in my twenties when I started to be out in public. At the time it didn't feel brave, it just felt correct. Back then I found it harder to get work in the theatre and even today I get messages from young actresses who find it hard and are scared to be out.

When I wrote my first crime novel Calendar Girl in 1993 it was unusual as I had written an out lesbian character (London-based private investigator Saz Martin) for whom being gay wasn't a problem. Those early crime novels were originally turned down by the Women's Press because I had included a lesbian villain. But Calendar Girl, Wavewalker, Beneath the Blonde, Fresh Flesh and Mouths of Babes were published by a mainstream independent publisher, Serpent's Tail. I was particularly proud that Calendar Girl was listed in the top five Big Gay Reads and was the only book in the top five that hadn't been adapted for television.

Having grown up in the sixties and seventies, I'm astonished that things have changed so quickly. I certainly didn't expect to be civilly-partnered and potentially married to Shelley, my wife of 23 years. However there is still a certain amount of ignorance and a fascination with lesbian lives as if we are somehow different. I don't believe we are, even if there are plenty of gay people who like feeling special and act like 'outsiders'. I think we change society sooner and better when we live inside it.

Our current need to define ourselves as lesbian, gay, heterosexual or bisexual in our teens is too early and just absurd. While some people might feel very clear about it, I think most young people – both heterosexual and homosexual – don't know what their sexuality is until they are in a relationship. We are asking young children to define their sexuality at an early age and it's impossible to do that until you have explored it more. In reality most LGBT people have had a sexual experience with the opposite sex, I did. Yet straight people rarely have and I think that's sad. If people were encouraged to be more fluid about their sexuality when they were younger it might lead to fewer broken marriages when one partner realises he or she is gay later in life and has to leave the (heterosexual) marriage. If more straight people were open about the occasional gay relationship they had, when they've slept with someone of the same sex once or twice, the percentage of 'gay' people would be much higher than five or ten per cent.

Your sexuality is not the most important thing about you. The world might tell you differently, but by the time you're in your 20s and 30s you realise what matters is your work, your friends and your family, and while sexuality is intrinsic to who you are, it's not the most important thing.

Stifyn Parri

Entertainer/producer
Born: Rhosllanerchrugog, near Wrexham, 1962

Best known as:
Playing gay character Christopher Duncan in the TV soap
Brookside and performing the role of Marius in *Les Miserables*
in London's West End. Founder of the Welsh ex-pats group
SWS (Social Welsh and Sexy). Now runs events and
production company MR PRODUCER.

Stifyn Parri

M y first gay kiss made the headlines on the 9 O'Clock news on the BBC. It was just a peck on the cheek but it was big news.

It was 1985 and I just got the part of Christopher Duncan in *Brookside*. It was my first mainstream TV role outside of my home country Wales. At the time *Brookside* had been running for three years and was one of the most watched soaps on TV. It was well-known for its controversial storylines. Everyone thinks the first gay kiss on TV soap was the lesbian one with Anna Friel but that came nine years after my *Brookside* screen kiss with 'Gordon Collins' and the *Eastenders* kiss with Michael Cashman was two years after ours.

There were two main families living in *Brookside* Close at the time, the Grants and the Collinses. The Grant family was headed by Bobby and Sheila (played by Ricky Tomlinson and Sue Johnston). Across the Close there was the Collins family, dad Paul, magistrate mum Annabelle and their two children Gordon and Lucy, who had been forced to downsize after Dad lost his job.

At the time I had graduated from London's Guildhall Music and Drama – or Mucus and Trauma as the students called it – and moved back to Cardiff where I had a job on a Welsh-speaking soap opera Coleg, which was the first programme on the newly-launched Welsh language channel S4C. I would watch *Brookside* and followed the storyline when the Collinses' teenage son Gordon came out as gay after his copy of *Gay Times* was delivered to one of the neighbours by mistake. As the story developed he went off to France to work and there was a hint that he had met a boy out there. I remember sitting in my flat in Cardiff on my orange shag pile rug one evening thinking, I wonder who will play his boyfriend?

Not long after that I got a call from my agent, a very 'old school' and proper lady, who said, 'You have an audition for Christopher's, ahem, 'friend'. I took the train from Cardiff to Liverpool, where the series was filmed and for five and a half hours I sat in front of the mirror in the toilet cubicle perfecting my Scouse accent. When I arrived at the audition there were lots of outrageously camp, pink-dungareed gay boys skipping around. And in the middle I stood, 6ft 3, chunky, with short, spiky hair. When it was my turn to audition, the casting director said, 'Do you realise this character's from Wrexham?'

'Well I am from a small village not far from Wrexham,' I replied. 'But you're telling me I've wasted the last five and a half hours on the train learning the most outrageously rude sentence in a Scouse accent?'

They said, 'We're terribly sorry, didn't your agent tell you? But let's hear your line anyway.'

I launched into 'Get your friggin' stockings off and let me f*** you, chicken,' and as I did the camera fell off the tripod and landed on the floor. Without thinking I followed the camera and lay down on the floor in front of it and that's how I finished the audition.

By the time I got home to Cardiff my agent rang to tell me I'd got the part. I later discovered that I looked like the sound guy on the programme, which was the type of actor they were looking for. The show's producers didn't know if he was gay or not and wanted someone slightly ambiguous and not the gay cliché.

"When I started working on *Brookside*, **I had not come out. Looking back it was a time when I actually was anti-gay gay because of the fear that I might be gay."**

I grew up in the village of Rhos, a close-knit mining village in north Wales, where it felt that most of the women in the village were over-the-top strong outrageous characters and the men were either hen-pecked or bruisers. I had various aunties, one sang opera and ran the local chip shop with my mother, another was a comic. Although it was tough and everyone judged everyone else, I never felt like I fitted in but I never wanted to fit in. My aim was to do as I wanted and keep my spirit happy and free. I liked standing out. I was creative and I was lucky to be allowed to be creative. On my first day of school, at the age of three, apparently I announced to the headmistress, 'I want to do a play on Friday'. I don't know where that idea came from. She said yes so I made up a play called the Spirit of Bryn Y Brain based on a local council estate. I played the lead, made the costumes out of my mother's curtains and took things from her house to make the set, and made my first public performance. Basically I did that all through school until I was 18 and went off to drama college. Looking back I realised I must have been gay at an early age. When I was five my best girl friend had her hair cut short and I cried because I couldn't brush her hair any more, so there was something going on there.

Yet as a teenager I had lots of girlfriends, I was never effeminate but more theatrical. I liked being different and was into Toyah Willcox. I wore big old gas coats to stand out. When I was 15 my dad died suddenly and gave me an insight into loss that many people don't experience until much later in life. After his death my relationship with my mother changed, she became more outrageous and we became closer and more like friends. When I left home and moved to London for drama college I had lots of girlfriends. In fact Neil Morrissey's girlfriend left him for me and he's never forgiven me because I later came out, but we are still friends.

When I started working on *Brookside*, the whole village of Rhos was proud of me. It didn't matter that I was playing a gay character as I had not come out. I was a local boy and I was being watched by millions of people every tea time. I was only meant to be in it for one episode but I ended up staying for two years. At the time *Brookside* was at the peak of its popularity. The writers cooked a really nice character for me in Christopher Duncan. He was a ski instructor, an antique dealer and a bit of a shit, but he was a loveable bastard. He got thrown out of the Collins' house 10 times because they were a strict family and he kept breaking their rules. He didn't get on with Gordon's gran but when she was being ill-treated in the old people's home Christopher went in and kidnapped her. Another time he bought the Collins family a lovely dog called Lucky. Ten weeks later he ran over it. He'd be asked to look after someone's house when they were on holiday and rent it out.

The gay kiss was such a huge fuss. It was nothing more than a peck on the cheek. Mark Burgess, the actor who played Gordon, and I rehearsed the scene beforehand. He was supposed to pin a badge on my jumper then lean in and kiss me on the cheek. All I remember is that he didn't put the badge in properly and when he pushed against me to kiss me the pin stuck in my nipple. So my lasting memory of that scene is not a kiss but a stab in the heart. It's weird because at the time it didn't mean anything to me, it was just a peck on the cheek, not even on the mouth. But suddenly it was all over the news because it was the first time that two gay men had never been seen being affectionate in a soap opera. Looking back now I do feel that I've been a part of something significantly important.

Later in the storyline Gordon and Christopher had a bed scene. At that time Mary Whitehouse was leading the National Viewers' and Listeners' Association, which campaigned against sex, violence, swearing and homosexuality on TV, and she had a book of rules. Our 'bed scene' only amounted to Gordon and Christopher in bed chatting. But the rule said that Mark and I both had to keep our jeans on under the duvet – as if there was any point in stripping off when we were only being filmed from the waist up. I had to lie on my back and Mark had to have his back turned towards me and face the wall.

"After the kiss I had loads of fan mail from gay men saying, 'Thank God, you're the only thing that keeps me going,' or, 'what you've been through has helped me enormously.'"

Other letters would start by saying I'm not gay but ... and the rest of the letter proved that they were. Girls would write, 'I know you're not gay really but I still fancy you, will you go out with me?'

In the first year on *Brookside* I was wary of having relationships with anyone as I was conscious that people were only taking notice of me because I was in a soap. Later I went out with a guy from the cast, but I was still wary of being found out. Playing a gay character was less of an issue for me than for my on-screen boyfriend, who was actually married with two children. They would get funny looks when they were seen out walking together as a family.

For me the major part of coming out was actually putting the words 'I am gay' into a sentence and telling my mother. I also wrote it in a letter to my brother and my best friend because I felt like I needed their approval. When I finally sat my mother down and told her I was gay she walked out of the room saying, 'No you're not.' I pleaded with her to listen to me. After about half an hour she settled down. I realised she was worried about what other people would think of me. It was all right for me to be playing a gay character on TV but as soon as people realised I was gay in real life, their attitudes would change and my mother's initial concern was to look after me. As soon as I told her I could look after myself and it was nothing that she should be ashamed of, she was proud of me. I then showed her a photograph of another famous actor, who she thought the world of, wearing a nightie to impersonate Shirley Bassey and once I told her he was gay too, that seemed to make it better. From that time we have become closer and when we are together she's camper than me.

In the two years I spent on *Brookside*, the writers came up with some cool gay storylines like the issue of gay men having to be Aids tested for mortgages, or coming home and seeing your house daubed with the word 'queer'. Another time it looked like Christopher and Gordon had been 'queer-bashed' coming out of a club. But in the next episode it was revealed that Christopher had hospitalised the guy who tried beating them up. The HIV testing later happened to me in real life as I did have to do various HIV tests for mortgages and having already dealt with it in *Brookside* it wasn't such a shock.

I have never felt that my sexuality has affected my career. I left *Brookside* and went into the West End musical Metropolis for nine months then I had the part of Marius in Les Miserables. My agent was never worried about me being gay, she was more concerned if I turned up for auditions wearing jeans instead of trousers. I have presented many series for BBC, ITV, S4C and Channel 4 and now I run my own events and talent agency in Cardiff and have worked with many celebrities and major events.

The only negative thing about being gay is being pigeon-holed. People tend to think my house will be full of glitter balls when it's not; or that my favourite singer is Liza Minnelli, when she's not. My pet hate is when some women say, 'You're such a waste.' I used to find it hurtful, now I actually find it insulting. I just think, why are you binning me? It upsets me more than men saying, 'Backs against the wall, boys.' I've learnt how to deal with those comments with humour, but to be called a waste when I think I've fulfilled so much and I go out of my way to live my life to the full is hurtful.

What I find bizarre now is that people don't need to come out. There's nothing to come out of. I wonder if that's better or not. I think you can gain strength of character by having to come to terms with something rather than be totally accepted. I feel I am a stronger person because of it.

Rosie Wilby

Comedienne and writer
Born: Liverpool, 1970

Best known as:
A Funny Women Finalist 2006 and has appeared on Radio
4 *Loose Ends*, *Midweek* and *Woman's Hour* and performed
at Latitude, Green Man and Glastonbury festivals and toured
several solo shows around the UK as well as appearances
in New York and Sydney. She's a former *Time Out* music
journalist and is currently writing a memoir about her brush
with minor Britpop fame. *www.rosiewilby.com*

Rosie Wilby

Steffi Graf's return hovers bee-like on the net cord and falls back ... on her own side. Yes!!! My mum is surprised I'm not supporting the young upstart. But how can she even be in the Wimbledon final? She's only a year and a bit older than me. Didn't she have to revise for exams? Still, justice prevails. Martina Navratilova leaps superwoman-like flying up into the air from the threadbare Centre Court lawn, as she equals some record held by someone from history I've never heard of. My own exams are done and dusted and I'm smug in the knowledge that I'm home and dry. Because I know I'm different, like Martina. This is a good thing. She is a winner. There is nobody else like us, except perhaps her friend that she hugs up in the player's box. Why do the commentators say 'friend' in such a weird way? They sound a little embarrassed. Later I videotape the BBC highlights montage and rewind and replay the scene where she hugs Chris Evert at the end of their semi-final. Set to music, it seems utterly romantic and makes me feel a bit swoony. I'm not sure which one I want to be.

My own superpower has not manifested itself in sporting excellence. That would be a big stretch, given the weedy physique of both of my parents. They even have small, weak cars as if to further demonstrate our family defects. A childhood ride in my dad's Mini Metro rendered even more humiliating by the addition of a 'Vote Kilroy Silk' banner across the back window, which ran above my head for years like an unwanted cartoon thought bubble. Fortunately in 1983 they abolished the constituency, he was no longer our MP and the banner has long since been removed. PE teacher Miss Bullock, also on my 'different' radar as she lives with a fellow tracksuit-clad woman in Whalley Drive, tries her best with me regardless of my challenged stature. My attempt at a Fosbury Flop in Games is disastrous, the high jump bar set so low that the girl with M.E. manages to faint over it.

Instead, my secret weapon is my brain. I try to play the fool to deflect attention from it, yet I fear my O Level results will give me away. We are the last year to do proper exams before some other piss easy system comes in. I think I may have fluffed my Art exam on purpose just to show a small sign of weakness so I'll still be accepted if I stay on in the sixth form. Who cares about drawing a sheep's skull on a grey, plastic table anyway? I've shot myself in the foot really because Art is the one thing I truly love. But time and time again I've been told it's not a proper subject. Not for a girl like me. The Grammar School has snobbery written through it like it's a stick of rock. It's a comprehensive now but clings on to the name as a last vestige of elitism. We all stand whenever the headmaster (or 'The Beak') enters the room. I occasionally do a quick impression in his chair just before everyone files in for Assembly. As I'm a girl who can work a sound system, I'm sometimes asked to set the microphone up for him. I agree just for the perk of backstage access.

For now, I just have these last few post-exam redundant days of summer term to get through unscathed, undiscovered. I spend as much as time as possible around JJ, kneeling at her desk with a handful of Thornton's Alpini, her favourites. I'm supposed to sit in my place but our form tutor, Mr Liver-sausage as we call him, doesn't care. He's a maverick. I like him. I don't dwell on his relationship with a girl our age, as she's in the lower academic stream and lives on the estate so she's not really one of us.

For two years now, I've given my unwanted feelings an elaborate system of secret codes. Every so often, I switch my attentions to a different girl just so I know I'm in control of it and not the other way round. I note her initials in my diary along with possible times and places for seemingly impromptu, yet incredibly staged, meetings based on her timetable. I've picked JJ mainly because she has the sort of cool older sister I wish I had and her best friend is a wet blanket who seems easily usurp-able. She also likes tennis, namely Stefan Edberg. But he looks like a girl so maybe there's hope. Most importantly, she is approachable, marooned somewhere between the trendy set with their perfectly asymmetrical bobbed hair, cheeky touch of electric blue mascara and fluffy ankle socks, and the make-up free squares with mullets and knee-length socks. Mine are even worse. They are navy blue. But, on Wednesdays, Mum gives me white socks to wear for Games and I feel thankful for this small way of feeling less apart, less marked out. When one of the trendy gang, Julia, is off sick I get to claim my rightful hockey place on the right wing. The bib bears my initials 'RW' which inspires me, tearing down the sidelines firing in drives for the centre forward to plop into goal past a half asleep keeper who can barely see for ridiculous padding and oversized helmet. Even Miss Bullock is impressed.

One night I am invited to stay over at JJ's house – sharing her tiny single bed! It is excruciating. I lie awake in the dark terrified to move in case I do anything inappropriate. Like me, JJ is an atheist and proudly says so in R.E. lessons to rebuff the proclamations of the tedious God-squad that all gay people are going to be rounded up on a desert island and shot. I think they're talking about men but, still, I must stay under the radar. I decide to accept a date with Darren Bond after he writes me an admiring note, signing it '007' – ironic really, as he reveals himself to be a much less effective secret agent than I. I love his long, floppy fringe, now recovered from a mishap with a Bunsen burner. It almost makes him look like a girl, or one of Wham! which is just as good.

Still, nothing happens on our aimless 'date' as we mooch around Ormskirk. It's an unsexy Lancashire town, famous for its market, clock tower and gingerbread. Unsexy, that is, until the arrival of Kevin the bisexual hairdresser and his salon De-Ziners. Not many people in Ormskirk know what the word bisexual means so Mum has to explain to other mothers that it's not the same as hermaphrodite. Kevin offers me a free perm on condition he can display a photo of it in the window. Yet, sadly, it's not the popular shaggy poodle perm but more of a curious mushroom shape that sits on top of my head. Once again, I've shot myself in the foot and marked myself out.

For the end of term, we have a French-themed entertainments evening. Our class put on an 'Allo 'Allo! sketch I've written casting Mr Liver-sausage, appropriately, as René. 'You're not the director, Rosie' moans one of the squares playing Michelle 'of the Resistance'. Fortunately she shall say this only once. My parents are visibly relieved that there is a simple explanation as to why I've been cutting out red paper Swastikas. I haven't joined an Ormskirk Nazi group. I'm playing Helga and am attaching the swastikas to my suspenders. Strangely, this is fine with them. After we rightfully bring the house down, a younger girl comes onstage in a French maid's outfit to sing 'Chansons D'Amour'. I am transfixed. She's a great singer but that's not the reason. I want to reach out and touch her ... and then what ...?

"Mum is on to me. One day, she pops out to the garage to get some fish out of the deep freezer and disturbs me basking on the front patio to say, 'I wouldn't mind if I had a daughter who was a lesbian.'"

She then proceeds to tell me something about her and her friend Joan on holiday. I'm not listening. I scowl. I'm not ready for this. It's my own private world. Maybe the neighbours can hear. She merrily pops back into the house to triumphantly return with a book of lesbian poetry. Later she reads from it at the tea table. What is she doing?? My dad and I shift uncomfortably, silently in our seats.

Maybe all my troubles started here in our road, The Serpentine. An oppressive looped cul-de-sac, it perfectly encapsulates my sense of being trapped. Each summer, however, the gang of bored local teenagers embrace its quirky shape and reclaim the circular section as our running track for 'The Serpentine Olympics'. Then in the warm evenings, we retreat to my mum's garage (we are a two-car family as my parents prefer to do separate things) and lazily wave around an old dustpan and brush under the guise that we are being helpful and 'cleaning' the garage. In fact, we are talking about sex. Ironic as in later life I pretend to be cleaning in order to avoid a discussion about sex. I have plenty to talk about the day I get stopped by a flasher. The Serpentine seems an odd location to choose given its lack of footfall, his efforts somewhat wasted on a fledgling lesbian (though obviously I don't mention that part).

Finally, on the last day of school, I see JJ ahead as we are all leaving. The devil in me takes over and I decide to catch her up and tell her everything.

'I'm sorry for being weird around you. I was in love with you. But, don't worry, I'm not any more'. She slows down, traumatised by this news and my flippant delivery of it, leaving me to skip, graceful and agile like Martina on Centre Court, out of the gates for the final time. I am free, for now, to be whatever I want to be.

Chris Needs

Radio Presenter
Born: Neath, Wales, 1954

Best known as:
His Sony Award-winning late-night radio show, *Chris Needs Friendly Garden,* which is broadcast six nights a week on BBC Radio Wales. In 2005 he was awarded an MBE for his charity work with the Chris Needs Hospital Appeal.

Chris Needs

I never really ever came out ... I was never in. I think I popped out of my mother's womb with a handbag in my hand.

I grew up in Port Talbot, south Wales, or what I call 'The Land of the Twitching Curtains', where I never fitted in. I was very much a loner. The other boys were interested in girls – I wasn't. They were into football – I wasn't. They were into woodwork – I wasn't. I would have preferred to learn how to cook. I was what the locals would call 'arty farty' and music was my big thing. I played the piano and took part in nativity plays at my local chapel and performed at Eisteddfodau, which are Welsh cultural festivals.

Living in such a small town in south Wales in the late 1950s and early 1960s, being gay was hard. I looked up to female impersonator Danny La Rue and watched Larry Grayson who presented on the TV show The Generation Game. I wanted to be like them. I was rather flamboyant as a teenager. Learning to play the piano was my way of expressing myself. I loved to watch Liberace with his grand piano, sequins and candelabrum and would mimic him.

"My mother always protected me. In her eyes I was always right and could do no wrong. She used to say she had three children – one of each."

But I was a disappointment to my father. He wanted me to go out with girls and play football and I said, 'No thank you.' I remember my father would say things to me like, 'Your mother made you a right floozy,' which was a slang term for a loose woman.' My reply would be, 'Good. Do you think she'll make one for my friend as well?'

From the age of seven I had an awful time. I was abused by a friend of the family, which should have put me off men really. He would take me up the mountain to pick wimberries and would assault me, telling me, 'If you tell your mother and father about this you'll go to borstal for being a queer.' I was afraid to tell them. I thought I was a naughty boy. It went on for years until, at the age of 13, I plucked up enough courage to stand up and threatened to go to the police and he backed off. The worst part of being a rape victim is the anger. I still live with this every day of my life. Luckily today there are organisations where children and abuse victims can get help and they don't have to suffer in silence.

I was not accepted by anybody. I was persecuted and beaten up for simply being alive. I was called queer and shirt-lifter. At 13 I even tried to hang myself because I was so depressed. When I was at comprehensive school I remember being given lines. I had to write, 'I am a nancy boy – I must change' 100 times. As I got older I would go to nightclubs and when I walked into the toilet the other men would say, 'Backs against the wall, boys.'

"When I was 18 I moved away from Wales to work as an entertainer in Holland and Spain. It was a great life. I saw other gay men and it was acceptable. No one laughed at me and no one gave me lines. It was my world. I was there for 22 years. Back in Wales I was treated like a clown."

I have spent my life covering up my unhappy childhood with comedy as best as I can. When I was younger I would hide behind camp jokes. Lots of people find gay men funny. I don't mind taking the mickey out of myself – but I don't like others doing it. As an entertainer in clubs and theatres

I would regularly get heckled and I developed some great put-down lines. If a man in the audience said something nasty to me I would simply say, 'You're safe as houses. It's only men I'm after,' or, 'I saw you in the toilet, ten tons of dynamite with a two-inch fuse.' That would certainly get their backs up and the laugh would be on them. At other times I have been performing in a club and overheard two men saying, 'What do you think of that bloody queer. Marvellous, isn't he?'

In 1989 I moved back to Wales and was given a weekly show at a local Cardiff radio station Touch FM. That's where I started my Friendly Garden Association and it grew in popularity. In 1996 I won a Sony Radio Award, which is the equivalent of an Oscar in the radio world, and my career went mental. I was offered a job by the BBC and I have been broadcasting every night ever since. The Chris Needs Friendly Garden grows daily. I have more than 50,000 members and each member has his or her own personal number and badge. We even have pets who are members. On air it's one big happy family with members calling in for a chat like old friends.

One listener phoned into my radio show and said, 'My nephew is the same denomination as you, love.' Comments like that are fine as it comes from the heart. I think today it's so much easier for gay people. When I was a kid you were jailed for homosexuality. Even after it was decriminalised in 1967 you had to be over 21. Now you can get married and have children. It's easier for gay people to be accepted. If someone is gay – it's cool.

"When I was a teenager I was called a stinking, horrible, warped, filthy queer. Now if someone calls you a rotten poofter they can be charged with an offence."

There's more acceptance towards gay young people today. I once gave a talk to a LGBT student group and they were shocked when I told them the names I got called as a young man. 'You can't say that,' they said. I told them, 'In my day it was not only acceptable, it was expected to be said.' Now you have rights and anti-gay abuse is treated the same as racial abuse but during my childhood gay people had no rights.

I still find it hard coming to terms with the way things have changed for the better. My partner Gabe and I have been together for 23 years and in 2013 we had a civil partnership. It was a beautiful day and it's the best thing I've ever done.

"But in the months leading up to the ceremony I thought, 'Two postmen and no letter-box: it's so wrong.' For the majority of my life that was the message that had been drummed into me was that homosexuality was wrong. That will never leave me."

Alice Arnold

Journalist
Born: Esher, Surrey, 1962

Best known as:
Former Radio 4 announcer and newsreader, she now writes
for the *Telegraph's* Wonder Women section on a range of
issues including: media, culture, gay rights and the law;
partner of Clare Balding.

Alice Arnold

I'm not one of those people who thought I was gay from an early age and that something was desperately wrong. I attended a private girls' school, where I played lacrosse to a fairly high level. I had crushes on coaches and players from other schools but at that age didn't really know what that meant. But I also had crushes on Donny Osmond and David Cassidy just like the other girls of my age.

My parents never assumed that I couldn't do anything because I was a girl. It was always assumed I would go to university and work and they encouraged me to take part in sport. At school there would be the odd comment that someone might be gay or lesbian but it wasn't a subject that was ever discussed. I did feel different to my peers but that was more to do with the fact that I cared about things like justice and inequality, racism and prejudice. While my friends were turning into Sloane Rangers, I became pretty left-wing and started challenging the system.

"During my school years I was going out with boys and was perfectly happy and didn't know there was any alternative. It wasn't until I got to Sussex University and fell in love with a woman that I realised what I had been missing was tummy flips."

I knew the woman in question was gay before I met her and she paid lots of attention to me, which I found incredibly exciting. At the time I didn't define myself as anything other than someone who had fallen in love with a woman. Like many people it was the person I fell in love with, the politics and identity followed later.

When I first came out to my friends at Sussex University it was considered really cool, no one thought it was odd or wrong. My family found out a bit later. They actually told me because they realised something was up. My mother was always fine about it but I didn't discuss it with my father until a time, much later, when I was in pain from a relationship and he showed me support. Although my parents were older, and are now in their 90s, they have always been completely supportive and accepting.

Clare and I had been friends for some time before we got together as a couple. We had been going out for a year or so when we were 'outed' in the press in 2003. We were attending a preview of the film *Seabiscuit* with Clare's parents, her brother and sister-in-law, when the press photographed us together.

The story that followed wasn't a shock to our family and friends as they all knew we were together. We had never ever denied our relationship, to do that would assume we were ashamed of it and we never were. The only thing we wouldn't do was have pictures taken together. According to the tabloid newspaper which ran the story, they knew Clare was gay because she went out with me. The consequent story that ran with the photograph was hilarious and full of absolute rubbish and made-up stuff. It said things like we wanted children, which we don't. That was difficult because people who read it, including our parents, thought it was true. We had to do a bit of repair work to reassure our friends and family that what they did originally know about us was correct and it was the paper that was wrong.

At first we weren't sure what sort of damage the story could do. We didn't worry or think that we'd lose our jobs because everyone at the BBC where we both worked knew we were a couple. Actually the ramifications of it for us were nothing. In some senses it made it easier as now everyone knew and we didn't have to try to hide things. I don't think there was any harm done at all. Although it has taken 11 years for the press not to mention that Clare is a lesbian, but by and large the experience didn't do any damage.

For some people there is still a huge dilemma over the fear of being outed in the press, some are afraid of losing their sponsorship, but the fear is greater than the actual damage. It is just tomorrow's chip paper. It's interesting how lots of people think being out could be negative and lose you money, whereas now I'm being asked to speak on diversity panels and host diversity events. I think people actually respect it and want to hear what I have to say. I'm not sure people would be interested in my voice if I wasn't Clare's partner. But because I am and I'm pretty outspoken about being gay and equal rights I think that opens a lot of positive opportunities.

"My advice to others is don't be afraid, don't be ashamed. Just be. Unless you have family who will be hurt on religious or homophobic grounds, there is nothing to be afraid of."

I know I speak from a privileged position as Clare and I are completely out where we live and work in London, whereas it may not be so easy in other parts of the country, but we have never come across any prejudice against us among our neighbours or when we go to places like banks or gyms. I find the more confident you are the less likely people will have derogatory thoughts. The more people who say, 'Yeah I'm gay, get over it,' the better. If you are out there and proud and happy, it's hard for people to say something nasty.

Shelley Silas

Writer
Born: Calcutta, India, 1959

Best known as:
Writer of radio and stage plays including *The Sound of Silence*, *Mr Jones Goes Driving* (for Richard Briers), a co adaptation of *The Raj Quartet*, *Calcutta Kosher*, *Mercy Fine*, *Falling*, *Eating Ice Cream on Gaza Beach* (2008). She also compiled and edited *12 Days*, an anthology of short stories.

Wife of Stella Duffy.

Shelley Silas

I had my first relationship with a woman at drama school, which was extraordinary because it's not what I expected. I had these feelings, they were comfortable feelings but very new. I wasn't sure what they were and I couldn't talk to anyone about it.

"Even if I'd wanted to there was no one. It was the late 1970s and it was still not acceptable to be gay, let alone openly so."

I had read Radclyffe Hall's The Well of Loneliness and Rita Mae Brown's Rubyfruit Jungle, all the classic coming-of-age lesbian books, as I tried to find something to identify with. I think a lot of the women in these books were stereotypical gay women and because of this they didn't represent me. I was searching for something else and I was fighting against it as it wasn't what I thought I should be. I had all the usual crushes on Martina Navratilova and Billie Jean King, but there was never a time when I thought 'I'm a lesbian'.

My dad was born in Calcutta, India and at the age of two moved with his family to Palestine where he later fought in the Israeli War of Independence. My mum left her wealthy family in India when she was 19 and moved to London, alone, lived in digs in West Hampstead and worked as a secretary. She met my dad in London through mutual friends. Both my parents are remarkable people, incredibly hard-working, down-to earth, generous and loving. Until their early eighties they ran their own book distribution business. They have been amazing role models to me and my sister, and brought me up to believe that I should be able to stand on my own two feet and look after myself. They are my heroes.

My sister and I were also born in Calcutta, but we came to London when I was two and she was four and we grew up in Golders Green, north London.

As a child I was a tomboy with long straight hair. I played with guns, disliked dolls, not that I think these are prerequisites for being a lesbian, and I used to ride up and down the road on my beloved orange Chopper bike. There's a photograph taken when I was around 12 years old. I am wearing a brown, shiny fake leather pinafore dress, which I adored. I refused to wear anything else. Looking back, I can see it was a horrendous piece of clothing and I must have driven my parents mad, but at that age I loved it. I used to wear it with desert boots and my hair in bunches. I resembled a little Calamity Jane, which is no bad thing!

I went to one of the country's first secondary modern schools. It was massive and I was miserable. Having left my small and safe primary school, I was really unhappy moving to this bigger environment. I was a dreadful student, I cried quite a lot of the time in my first year, and the teachers had to call my sister out of her classes to come and look after me.

I couldn't sit and focus, I didn't care about school, all I was interested in was going to the theatre because I wanted to be an actress and star in musicals. I loved musicals and hung around with like-minded people. I wanted to play Nancy in a school production of *Oliver!* But because I'd had my hair cut short, the part went to another girl, who had waist length hair. I had the better voice. Who knows, my career might have been very different had the part been mine.

Because I was from an immigrant family, I didn't really get on with the Eastern European Jews in my school; we, the Sephardis, were seen as 'other'. Subsequently, most of my friends were not Jewish. And because I mixed with so many people, the most important lesson I gained from school was learning to tolerate people who were different to me. I was introduced to all classes, nationalities and religions, which set me up to be accepting of other people. I never questioned anyone about the way they were or what they were. It's why I am still against private schools and faith schools. Ghettos create barriers instead of breaking them down. My school photo has such a cross-section of colours and ethnicities, I am proud of that special gift my school gave me. Much as they wanted to, I'm really glad my parents couldn't afford to send me to a private school. I probably would have ended up a very different person. My school allowed me to be the person I am today.

At school I had the classic young girl crushes on a couple of female teachers and I didn't think anything of it, because I wasn't the only one who felt this way. Besides, I always expected to marry a nice Jewish boy. I did have relationships with men and at school I always liked the boys who didn't like me, but ultimately my heart and soul felt more comfortable with women. It didn't make sense then, as a schoolgirl, it was only at drama school where I had my first relationship with a woman, that everything fell into place.

I had several boyfriends and if it had worked out I might have settled down with one of them, but, for whatever reason, it didn't work out. It's not that I'm not attracted to men, I'm more attracted to women.

When I was in my late twenties I met a woman who I thought was going to be the love of my life. I remember having a party for my 30th birthday. This woman was there and so were my parents.

Some of my friends knew about our relationship and they were all supportive but I wasn't out to my parents.

"During the party my dad sensed something was going on between the two of us. When he found out he said he was going to kill us both. He was really angry and during a phone conversation, he said, 'I need help. I don't know how to be, I don't know what to do.'"

Some time after that the relationship ended, which was a good thing, and I met Stella.

It was the autumn of 1990. A mutual friend had taken me to see an improv show at the Banana Cabaret in Balham, where Stella was performing. The first time I saw her on stage I fell in love with her. I remember it well. I had recently had my long hair cut short for a Liza Minnelli look-alike shoot for the magazine I had been working for. Stella wore red Converse and her hair was a mass of red too. I offered to drive her home, but she said no. I called her a couple of nights later but her flatmate didn't pass on my message. I persisted, called again, and eventually we went out. From our first date I knew she was my soul mate.

We moved into my flat in north London, but the fear of bumping into my parents was constant. I lived in flat with my first cousins living above and below me. Even though most of my family knew about our relationship, no one spoke about it because they didn't want to upset my parents. In order to have an easier life we rented my flat and moved to south London.

To Stella's credit she never once told me not to see my parents, she always encouraged me to have a relationship with them, though at times the pain was unbearable. She never made me choose, them or her. We were both invited to various birthday parties and family occasions by relatives, but I refused to go without Stella because we should have gone as a couple, like everyone else, but I had assumed it would have been too uncomfortable. I did go to Friday night dinners at my parents and the festivals by myself, but eventually, I realised that by doing so I was condoning their actions. At the time it felt like the only way. I should have stopped going years earlier, maybe change would have come sooner.

Then Christmas 1999 arrived and Stella and I had invited my sister and her children to our house for lunch. When my niece and nephews were younger they always used to enjoy decorating our Christmas tree because they never had one. Stella suggested I invite my parents. I didn't want to, I was tired of rejection, I didn't see the point. But Stella encouraged me to give them another go.

Trembling, I picked up the phone and called my dad. I said, 'Look, Dad, no one's died, no one's ill, it's about to be a new millennium, we're not drug addicts, we're not murderers. Everyone knows about Stella and nobody cares, so we'd love you to come for lunch with Leah and the kids.'

He was silent and then said, 'Let me think about it.'

Stella and I were going to Venice for the weekend. I was anxious the entire time, waiting for our return and a response.

While we were away, my dad had taken my sister out for lunch and discussed it with her. She said to him, 'You know what you have to do.'

We returned from Venice and my dad called to say they were coming for lunch.

We booked a table at a local restaurant and in the run-up

to their arrival we were really nervous but the minute they walked into our home, it felt like we had been blessed. There was no animosity, no hatred, no resentment, nothing. Stella had made mince pies because she knew my mother loved them. My parents were due to go to New Zealand, Stella gave them a map for their holiday, she'd grown up there after all.

The nine years of difficulty disappeared and since then we have mostly been a happy family. My sister died two years ago, which has been the most unbearable loss in our lives. My nephew has had a baby and my niece came out.

"My parents talk about Stella like their third daughter. My mother also apologised to Stella for giving her such a hard time. She often says 'We have had more joy and respect from Stella than we ever had from your sister's ex-husband.'"

I realise that if my parents had met Stella earlier in our relationship my father might have come around sooner, but part of me was probably ashamed or scared or worried about being judged, and so it was easier in a way for them not to meet. The biggest fear that kept me awake at night was that something would happen to my parents or Stella and the three most important people in my life would never have met. I used to cry over it. Despite all the difficulties, my dad refusing to come to my graduation and my mum trying her hardest but always being loyal to her husband, they are now great friends, the kind of friends I could never have imagined. My dad loves cooking and gardening, so does Stella, she is one of the family.

A few years ago my dad, who is a computer expert, created a family tree. We all sat down to watch, and there was Stella, as my life partner. I cried. It's wonderful for me that they are all in each other's lives and that finally they all realise how important they are to me and now to each other.

When Stella and I had our civil registration party in 2005, my parents came. Our family and friends were there, including the Duffys who have always been brilliant about our relationship. Sadly Stella's mother, Peg, had already died. Her absence was great. I had enormous respect for Peg, she loved me from the moment we met, never judged me, just asked me to look after her daughter. The last time we were all together was on Father's Day at my parents' house, another impossibility made a reality. My mother always calls Peg a real lady. At our party, my dad made a speech. I'll never forget his words. He said 'I got one daughter and I got another one for free.' It was gorgeous and meant so much to me. It was a real acknowledgement of his acceptance. At our legal civil partnership, my parents travelled to Brixton at 9 a.m. on a Friday morning and were part of our small group. They witnessed our history taking place.

Looking back to the difficult days, my dad simply didn't know what to think and how to react. He believed there was only one way to be. Having a gay daughter was new to him, he was scared of what people would say. As soon as he accepted it he expected everyone else to be okay about it. The truth was, they already were. My mum is almost 85, and my dad almost 86. They talk about gay rights in a way I never thought possible. Having a gay child has changed them and made them think about things in a different way, it's made them aware of other people's needs. I recently had a conversation with my dad about the difference between civil partnership and marriage. I sent him a link to my blog. They both know that equality is vital for everyone.

My advice to young people who are scared of coming out to their family is that you don't know how your parents are going to respond. In your head you may have decided they are going to be negative and angry, but you don't know for sure. It's no one right to out anyone, but in my experience, it's a weight taken off your shoulders, a weight you should not have to carry. Not being who you are is hard. It's hard for a lot of young people especially those from religious backgrounds who are worried about losing their families. But every family is different and I know religious people who are out and their families cope. Be true to yourself and don't lie about who you are, let it be someone else's problem. In the end you are only hurting yourself and you don't deserve to be hurt. And never second-guess how someone will respond. My very religious uncle had always been kind to us. He adored Stella, he used to send her notes from the bible. He never once rejected us. Miracles do happen. I know not everyone has as happy an ending as me, I'm aware that there are others who are still not accepted, but the only way to make it better for each other is to be true to yourself, by doing that we build a future where we can be safe and accepted.

Phyllis Opoku-Gyimah

Executive Director of UK Black Pride
Born North London, 1972

Best known as:
Co-founder and Executive Director of UK Black Pride, ranked
11 in *the Independent*'s Top 100 Pink list and 72 in the
Guardian's World Pride Power List 2013. Phyllis is Head
of Campaigns and Parliamentary Affairs for the Public and
Commercial Services (PCS) Trade Union, a member of the
TUC LGBT Committee and a board member of Justice for
Gay Africans which focuses on Human Rights, Equal Rights,
challenging racism and discrimination.

Phyllis Opoku-Gyimah

I was in primary school when I first realised I might be gay. I had finished a PE lesson and this girl kept on teasing me, telling me how much she liked my new plimsolls. I knew that I liked her but could not explain the funny tummy feeling. Despite that I suppressed the feelings for many years until my adulthood.

I grew up in in Islington, north London up until the age of 13, then moved to an all-white neighbourhood in Hertfordshire, I was really a good girl. But as soon as I hit my teens my studies took a back seat. I was battling with racism and prejudice in school, where I was the only black girl. I remember seeing members of the National Front marching through our streets in Waltham Cross calling out names like 'nigger,' 'Paki' and 'faggot' and it was scary, nerve-wracking, but very difficult to explain, I felt like I didn't belong and those people did not want me around them, in their shops, or in their school.

"It was very sad and now, when I reflect back, I wish I could have said something. But at the age of 13, you don't want to get your head kicked in, especially if you already feel that there's nobody around that understands you."

My parents were both from Ghana and very strict Christians, so religion played a major role in my upbringing. They encouraged me to do well in school. I came out with good grades ,but I wish they would have been a bit more liberal and talked to me about diversity of people like gays, lesbians, bisexuals and transgendered. In our household there was never any realisation of gay people apart from watching Kenny Everett and Freddie Mercury from Queen on television. But even then I don't think I realised it was a gay thing. As I got older I became more influenced by performers like Tracy Chapman, George Michael and Joan Armatrading. I lost myself in music; it was my drug.

I wouldn't change a single thing about how I was raised, but especially all the tough moments in a very religious household; even having to go to church and hear the pastor preaching about how sinful and immoral it is to have people of the same gender believing that they can be together, shouting, "It's wrong, wrong, wrong ..."

For many years I tried to be the person my parents wanted me to be – conforming to what they believed was right in society, obey your husband, have children, cook and clean and the rest. Then, nearly 19 years ago when I could take no more of living a lie, I decided to do something about it – I found the courage, the confidence, the faith and belief in myself that I am allowed to be ...

"At first I was worried about how my family would accept the news given their religious background. Also I had children and I had to ensure that they did not get caught up in my decision to come out."

Initially, different people reacted differently to me. When I told my mum there was a sense of shock, horror, disbelief and anger. She told me she was, 'very disgusted as I had bought shame on the family'. Some of my close friends were more accepting than others. Out of the five friends I told, three stood by me and supported me. But someone who was close to me hurt me physically, mentally and emotionally, seeing me as making a choice to be a lesbian, when really I made a choice to be me. It was very painful to deal with at the time but now I am stronger and better for the journey

I have been on. My journey has not been an easy one, due to many barriers and obstacles arising from my multiple identities as being black, a woman, a mother, a lesbian, a worker, and someone with a hidden disability, but I would not change one single thing. Because every day I grow and am able to instil good morals and standards in my family, it all starts with respecting people's difference.

Since coming out I have had so many positive experiences. There are many people who have contacted me through email, Facebook, and in person, and told me that, as a black woman who has come out, they are inspired by me. Some people have told me that my journey has given them power for their own journey; others say I have helped them to feel that they are ready to come out, black women who have children, who may be from Ghana, young women and men who are in college or uni wanting to know about various group or just organisations wanting me to come and speak at their events and networking groups.

Being part of the UK Black Pride event which celebrates LGBTQI (Lesbian, Gay, Bisexual, Transgender, Queer or Questioning, and Intersex) I am constantly reminded why I did come out and do what I do. We held our first Black Pride event in London in 2006 and since that day it has gone down in LGBT history as the leading celebration of African, Asian, Caribbean, Middle Eastern and Latin American LGBT people from Britain, Europe and internationally.

The team of 12 volunteers, all from the black communities, has been committed to growing the event so it has now become a permanent feature on the annual calendar of Pride activities and has grown from strength to strength as it secures the confidence, respect and support of the community, our friends and families. We have maintained the core essence of being the only Black LGBT community Pride event to be genuinely designed, delivered and led by the full diversity of Black LGBT people. It has also attracted support from around the world and a cross-section of society, including Members of Parliament, trade unions, Black and LGBT community and voluntary groups, providers of public services like the police and primary care trusts, as well as young people and students. Most importantly though, UK Black Pride continues to be supported by the community it serves to ensure the principle of 'Pride before Profit' and to guarantee UK Black Pride remains an inclusive event for all in our community. In 2011 UK Black Pride won a top prize in the Pink Paper's Readers' Awards.

"As Trustee and Executive director of UK Black Pride I feel as if I am now constantly coming out at every event I am invited to speak at. I do it because I want to be visible, seen and heard – as I am no longer scared."

I still encounter people who hold prejudices but I believe the way to turn that around is about education, constantly raising awareness and ensuring there is positive representation and are great role models in our community. There is a lack of visible black LGBT people, and although this may sound strange it is not just about race and being gay. When I was growing up I felt lost as there wasn't really a person that I could fully relate to or had the shared commonality, or struggle. The reason I am now so open and outspoken is because I want others who feel lost or feel that there is nobody like them to know there is.

My advice to others, from all backgrounds, who may be struggling to express their sexuality, is to be strong. You have to understand that not everyone is going to be happy for you on your journey, there are some negative and hateful people in this world but there are more positive and loving people who will support and love you for who you are.

Importantly, there are some great groups you can join and there are brilliant role models who share and understand what you are going through. Just keep on keeping on, don't let anyone dim your light!

Nigel Owens

International rugby referee; TV presenter
Born: Camarthen, 1971

Best known as:
Elite referee and first professional sportsman to come out in
the world of rugby union; TV presenter

Nigel Owens

I was 19 when I realised that I was different to the norm and from the other people around me. It was frightening as I didn't really know what a gay person was or looked like.

I grew up in Mynyddcerrig, a small village in Carmarthenshire in West Wales. It was a typical old-fashioned, close-knit farming community. My grandparents had a small farm, I went to Sunday school and chapel, and I grew up believing in Jesus Christ. The only time I ever heard the word gay used was in association with people who worked on the airlines as 'trolley dollies' or men who worked in hairdressing. I worked on a farm and farming wasn't the type of industry associated with gay men. I knew that gay people existed, but I had never seen one and didn't know anyone who was gay.

"I remember one time I walked into town and made a point of looking in through the hairdresser's window, I guess I just wanted to see another gay person."

Once I realised I might be gay, it was all quite new to me and I fought against it. For the first couple of years I had a girlfriend and tried to hide it but that only pushed me into depression. At the time I was working as a technician in local school and I had started refereeing local rugby matches, but inside I was fighting against my feelings. Being gay was something quite alien to the way I was brought up, which was to have a wife, have children ... I thought that was how the world had to be.

When I was 21 I had my first relationship with a guy, but I had to keep it a secret as I didn't want anyone to know. I was scared of what people would think if they found out and that made me even more depressed. I didn't want to be gay. I was worried about what my family would say, what my colleagues in the rugby world would say. I was also taking steroids at the time and it just got to the point where I couldn't cope with it anymore and wanted to take my own life. I was also bulimic at this time due to the fact I didn't like the way I looked. I did something I will regret for the rest of my life. I wrote a note to my mum and dad that said 'I just can't deal with it any more,' and went up onto the mountain with a bottle of sleeping tablets and a shotgun to kill myself. The tablets put me in a coma and actually saved my life. If it wasn't for that I have no doubt I would have pulled the trigger. I was found in time and airlifted to hospital, where I stayed for four or five days.

I was given a second chance.

After that I grew up a lot. My biggest challenge then was accepting who I was. Once I had done that, the next issue was: what was I going to do about it? I had a choice of either carrying on and hoping no-one would find out or come out. It was on my mind and I couldn't hide it anymore, so I made the decision to tell the people who cared for me.

First I told my mum, then one of my cousins and a couple of days later I told my friends. A lot of my friends were surprised. They said, 'Are you really gay? You don't look gay or act gay.' My family and friends were supportive and still are. Some older family members just don't talk about it but they still care for me like they've always done. I don't push it in their face. If people want to know, I tell them; if they don't, I won't.

After telling my family, there was another issue. Would I be able to carry on in the rugby world?

I was working with the Welsh Rugby Union and had refereed at international level. I was hoping to make my debut at the Rugby World Cup in 2007, I needed to know if I was going to be able to carry on with my job if I came out. If I wasn't able to do that I would have had to make the choice of either giving up refereeing, or carrying on as I was and hiding my sexuality.

When I came out to my boss at the WRU in 2007, he and all at the WRU were very was supportive and remain so till this day. Since then a few other sports people, who you would never have guessed were gay, have come out. It gives the message that you could be camp, straight-acting, tall or short: you're not gay because you're a certain type of person.

I do get abuse shouted at me during matches from time to time but a lot of it is banter and it's up to the individual to decide what they think is acceptable. I don't take it personally, it's part of the game for the referee to get abuse. Since coming out I have noticed that some people who are gay but who are not out don't want to be seen with me in public case they are found out to be gay by association. I understand totally how difficult it is for them, as not so long ago I was one of them and felt exactly the same. In sport I have found a lot of people who are gay, but most are in the closet and will probably never come out. There is nothing wrong with that as long as they are happy themselves, because that's what really matters. No-one should come out because they think they have to or should do to help others: you come out because it's right for you, and then you will help others just by being you.

"To me, the rugby world has been encouraging and welcoming, allowing me to deal with who I was, but I can also understand that people find it difficult."

Some sports still have a long way to go before they catch up with other parts of society in terms of being welcoming to gay, bisexual and lesbian people. Football is one of those sports where it's still very hard as we don't have any current players who are out.

In my experience coming out didn't make me any different or better at my job, it just enabled me to be myself. The fact I was happy in myself meant I could enjoy life and as a result I enjoyed my work. I had the opportunity to referee at the Rugby World Cup in 2007, not because I was gay, but because I was the best person for that job. If I had still been in the closet, I doubt that I would have been as relaxed in my work and therefore I wouldn't have been as able to do my job so well.

My advice to young people is to be yourself. The biggest challenge is accepting yourself. Only when you've done that can you move on. If you feel you need to come out to be yourself then it's OK to do so. No matter how frightening it may seem, people will accept you. There may be a rough ride ahead, but come out for the right reason: because you want to; don't feel you have to. Once you have accepted who you are, life is good. Only after you have become who you are can you say that life is what you make it.

Charlie Condou

Actor, Writer
Born London, 1973

Best known as:
For playing midwife Marcus Dent in the soap *Coronation Street* and being a 'celebrity gay dad'.

Charlie Condou

In my experience the hardest part of coming out was dealing with the fear that I would never have kids. For as long as I can remember I'd wanted to be a dad. I have a memory of coming home from nursery at the age of four in tears because I was never picked to bath the dollies at the end of the day.

When I was 18 I told my mother I was gay. It was not the traumatic experience it is for some as I was brought up in an unconventional and forward-thinking family living in Soho in the centre of London. Up until that point I had had girlfriends; it was just as I got older I realised I was more and more attracted to men and less and less to women. I don't remember having any big wake-up call, it just naturally happened.

"When I told my mum I had a boyfriend she was not surprised or upset. 'But you've always wanted to be a parent,' was her main concern. Back then gay parenting didn't exist, at least not in any public way."

There were men, often estranged from their kids, who had tried marriage in their 20s before coming out and leaving their families. But to see gay men in loving relationships, raising children together and building families was unheard of. But even at that age I knew I would have a family one day and couldn't see why being gay was going to stop that happening.

My mother loved my sister and me ferociously and taught us that whatever else life threw at you, whatever changes you went through, the love of a parent for a child was life's one constant. Having kids was not so much a goal, as an assumption. After coming out there was no obvious path to a family that I could follow: surrogacy was in its infancy, even for straight couples, and gay men were still considered too deviant to adopt. Around this time my sister told me 'When something is this important to you, you'll find a way.' I tucked that certainty away and got on with my life.

I met my friend Catherine in 1998 when she was dating a friend of mine. One night over dinner she said that, if she were still single when she got to 40, we should have a kid together. It was not a flippant comment, she was serious. We talked about kids and parenting and shared ideas about how children should be raised and what was important. As Catherine approached 40, I had been with my partner Cameron for six years and was happy with the idea of us starting a family. After years of talks, discussions and worst-case scenarios, Catherine and I embarked on IVF. One year and three cycles of IVF later, Georgia was born. For the first three months Catherine lived with Cam and I and we shared the responsibilities, then Catherine moved back to her own home which is near ours and Georgia has split her time between the two homes ever since. Georgia has three parents; Cam is as much a dad as I am.

The role of Marcus Dent in *Coronation Street* came in 2007, three years before our first child was born. At the audition I recognised a lot of gay actors. The casting directors seemed to be looking for an openly gay actor to play Marcus so in a weird way being gay helped me get the part. There has never been a question of me being OUT, I have never gone into casting auditions shouting 'I'm gay!' but it has never occurred to me to keep it a secret either. I'm not a particularly camp man so unless I talk about it people don't assume I'm gay. The fact that my character was gay wasn't a concern for me. Before *Coronation Street* most of my acting roles were playing heterosexual characters, drug dealers, homeless kids or soldiers. Before I accepted the role I thought long and hard whether I wanted to go into a long running serial like *Corrie* and commit to such a long contract.

The irony is that my character Marcus is now straight. But as he is such a nice guy people respond really well to him and as a result people respond really well to me. I have never had any abuse. I've had lots of letters from gay men saying it's nice to see someone on television that seems a bit like them. Marcus is emotionally intelligent and is committed to the person he's with so the viewers like him – even when he started his current relationship with Maria the hairdresser, the gay community stuck with him as they see Marcus as still being a gay character and I think even Marcus identifies as a gay man.

I was pleased to be involved in the gay parenting storyline with my on-screen boyfriend Sean. It made such a big difference as these shows have an impact, and play an important role in demystifying, and promoting tolerance. Catherine's father understood our arrangement immediately because he had heard the same situation played out on The Archers.

As the storyline between Marcus and Maria was first being developed, the scriptwriters, who were both gay men, talked to me about it. They wanted to look at what happened when a gay man who is comfortable with his sexuality falls in love with a woman. If we had played that story line 10 or 20 years ago then I probably would have had a problem with it. But I think we have genuinely moved on. I don't think people are as ignorant as to believe that all that Marcus needed was the love of a good woman. Some people make comments that the story is not realistic and we are giving the wrong kind of message. But I think we're giving the message that sometimes a person's sexuality is more complicated than gay or straight. I think it's really brave of *Corrie* actually to say 'this man has this sexuality, and it's a really complicated sexuality'. I encounter bi-phobia a lot; surprisingly most of it comes from the gay community who you would expect to be more accepting. I was once on a discussion panel with gay musician Tom Robinson, who wrote the gay anthem 'Glad to be Gay' in the early 1980s then fell in love with a woman a few years later. He still considers himself a gay man and is living proof that the Marcus/Maria storyline can and does happen. I would also consider myself a gay man, I have been with my partner Cameron for eight years, I'm not attracted to women and I don't imagine I will be, but that doesn't mean to say all gay men are like that sometimes the definition is more blurred. I imagine there will come a time on the Street when Maria and Marcus split up because he's gay but that's only my personal feelings – the scriptwriters never tell me where they are taking the storylines.

When the Daily Mail published a column by writer Brian Sewell attacking *Coronation Street* for being 'too gay' my career as a writer began. The day after his comment ran, I wrote in defence of *Corrie* arguing that 'aside from the barely-veiled homophobia' Brian Sewell was plain wrong. At the time there were just four regular gay characters in the soap, my character Marcus and boyfriend Sean, and teenager Sophie Webster and her girlfriend Sian, which out of 65 was not excessive. My comment was published in The Guardian, and from that I was offered my own weekly column – The Three of Us. It followed the pregnancy and arrival of my son Hal, who was born in January 2012.

Since then I have been labelled as a 'gay celebrity dad' and I'm happy with that. I am a dad, my work on *Coronation Street* has made me a celebrity, and I'm gay. Recently I have been approached by a women's magazine which is looking for a dad's voice in the magazine. They approached me because they liked my writing and I'm a dad, not because I'm a gay dad. I'm happy that I am now getting asked to comment as a father not simply a gay father.

I used to have a fantasy about being a father. I would gently lift my sleeping child from the car and carrying him or her upstairs to bed. I would imagine the small weight in my arms and the soft breath on my neck. I can't count the times I've re-enacted this scenario for real. And it feels exactly as I imagined it would. Having my children have not given my life meaning, my life was already meaningful, but the sense of responsibility I have now makes me feel more of a man somehow; maybe more adult is a better way of describing it. I understand what it is to put someone else first, to know that you love them more than they will ever love you, and that's as it should be. I'm a dad, and it just feels right.

As a parent you realise very quickly that no matter what you want from your children or who you would like them to be you have no influence over that. You can guide them and advise them but you cannot change them. My son is only one year old but he has a strong personality and I don't imagine I can do anything about that.

"If your child is gay and you're not comfortable with it there's nothing you can do. You have two alternatives: clash with them and probably lose them or try and support them and offer the love and understanding that a parent can."

Jade Ellis

Singer
Born: North London, 1987

Best known as:
X Factor Finalist 2012

Jade Ellis

When I was growing up in Greenwich I knew quite a few older lesbians. But if I'm completely honest if had taken what they showed me to heart I think I would have ended up asexual. Most of the same-sex couples I knew were in a state of constant dramas and problems.

My own childhood was great. My mother was a single parent and raised me and my brothers and sisters to just be ourselves and be happy. As a result I had a happy and carefree adolescence.

"I knew from a very young age that I was gay. Whenever I played kiss chase at school I kissed girls just as naturally as I kissed boys. One time I was called into the office at school to explain the love bites I had given a female mate during some experimenting. Needless to say this scared the life outta me and I remained silent about my female attractions until my early teens."

Throughout school I had several crushes. I used to idolise Madonna on MTV but I was more interested in the skimpy clothes and the sexy videos. I think started my Latino/Hispanic lady fascination started when I first saw Madonna her in the video for 'La Isla Bonita'.

At the age of 14 my 'gaydar' was all over the shop. I had a PE teacher who I knew was a lesbian She was really nice to me and encouraged my love for sports and made me feel like it was OK to be tomboy-ish when all the other girls my age were into hair and boys.

Living at home during my late teens, my sexuality just wasn't discussed. I brought ladies home and I know my mum had questions but I didn't feel I needed to have the conversation or the big "coming out" until I had a serious girlfriend. So one night when I was 17 the lady I was seeing stayed as per usual and when she left in the morning my mum said quite naturally, 'She is a pretty girl, very tomboyish ... is she gay?' I just said, 'Yes, Mum, she is and so am I,' to which my mum said, 'Oh OK ... do you want a cup of tea?'

Not really a coming-out more like just stating the obvious!

There was no frightening or worrying build-up to my coming out. I had already accepted that if my friends were off with me I would not consider them my mates. But luckily only one or two started acting strange and not wanting to get drunk around me like I was gonna attack them when they were vulnerable and I remember thinking, you wish.

When my girlfriend Heba and I met in 2006 I had been on the London 'scene' for about four years struggling to even find someone remotely ready or mature enough for a relationship. Everyone just wanted to get drunk, take drugs and have sex, which I was so bored with and past! I had just about given up on finding a normal, uncomplicated girl when I meet Heba at Bootylicious club in London. It was not the best situation to meet, my ex-girlfriend was there giving me evils, Heba's ex was giving her evils but we laughed the night away and soon became inseparable. So far, so good. Now all I had to do was explain my five-month-old daughter Caiden. After meeting Heba we became a close family. Caiden doesn't have two mums, she has one mum, a dad and Heba. We play different roles. Heba is a step-parent. And the people at school and in the community are fine about it. The other kids guessed before the parents in fact. The children would say, "hello, Caiden's mummies", whenever they saw Heba and me together, whereas the parents would constantly ask if Heba was my sister or cousin but deep down just like the kids they knew. To my knowledge there has never been an issue with the other parents at school accepting my sexuality, and, more to the point, we wouldn't care if they did have a problem with it.

When I entered X Factor in 2012 I hadn't sung since Caiden was born. I went to the audition at the 02 Arena in London with the aim of making a better life for us all. I was working as an assistant in a bike shop and although I enjoyed my job, I wanted to show my daughter, that it was OK to follow your dreams. Just being flown first-class out to St Lucia to the judge Tulisa's house was an experience.

My only worry about doing a show like X Factor was being put in the media spotlight.

"I thought it would be hard on Heba because she comes from a Muslim family and the pressure she has to conform is epic."

However her close family members have been there for her and the ones that don't like it didn't like it anyway so it didn't make any difference. That worry all turned out to be for nothing.

In fact I felt that our relationship was edited out or purposely overlooked. With so many outwardly gay participants in the finals, including Rylan Clarke, Lucy Spraggan and Charlie Rundle from MK1, the feminine lesbian was just not newsworthy enough. Although there were lots of exaggerated stories printed about me in the tabloids at the time. The most ridiculous was that I fancied Charlie. It was just a lazy story really and we saw it coming weeks before, just because we both like ladies. She is a beautiful girl and we want to collaborate as artists but that does not mean that we instantly like each other. When that story broke we were able to laugh about it.

Being a lesbian was never a problem for me on X Factor as I never really talked about it. When I lost out to the boy band Union J in the fourth week of the finals, I don't think being gay had anything to do with it. It was nice to have the support of the lesbian community behind me but I don't think that people didn't vote for me because I was a lesbian. Some people didn't even know that I gay so it was not a factor. In showbiz a person's sexuality is not big enough news to cause a stir nowadays.

The X Factor has given me quality time with my daughter, something I have not had since she was six months old. I am spending time in the studio recording new songs and I hope to release an album and go out on tour to play small venues. I feel I am showing Caiden that with hard work, love and support you can do anything.

People change and lives evolve, however, I can say that I know my sexuality will always be a part of me just as it always has been no matter what else changes. I find that strangely comforting.

My advice to other young lesbians is don't think about it really, be young, happy, and safe. You will always be who you are and if you try to hide it, you will make yourself and everyone around you confused and miserable. I know that life is different for everyone but just talk to the ones that love you and follow your heart.

Edd Kimber

Baker, Author
Born: Bradford,1985

Best-known for Winning
the first series of *The
Great British Bake Off* in
2010. A regular at food
festivals, he has written
two cookbooks *The Boy
Who Bakes* and *Say It
With Cake.*.

Edd Kimber

B efore taking part in The Great British Bake Off I had to sit with a psychologist. 'Are there any skeletons in your closet?' he asked, 'What if the question of being gay comes up? The newspapers might make something of it if the show becomes big.' I replied,

"'I have spent 20 years not being who I am so I'm not going to shut up and hide anything now. If it becomes an issue it's an issue. It's who I am.'"

When I entered the Bake Off I was stuck in a rut, I was working as a debt collector for a bank in Yorkshire, where I would get death threats on a daily basis. My way of escape was to think about new recipes and flavours for cakes, that's what kept me going through the boring days. So I was lucky to be chosen from 4000 applicants for the first series. Before the filming started all the contestants had to sit with the psychologist to find out if they were mentally capable of dealing with the stress the show and the press coverage could bring. At the time there were no other gay people in the series to my knowledge. Since 2010 there have been at least two gay men in every series and the 2012 winner John Thwaite is also gay.

As a child I had always felt different to other children, but never really understood why. I was always aware to some degree that I didn't feel the same as everyone around me I just didn't realise what that was until I was 12.

I had a normal, loving childhood. My parents were both self-employed antique dealers and spent time at home.

Our family's focal point mainly revolved around food and baking. One of my first memories is making mince pies with my mum. I was five at the time and she allowed me to cut out around the pastry. For my birthdays Mum would always bake cakes. Back then I never thought of baking as a hobby or a career, it was something we did together as an activity.

My parents were religious and we always went to church on a Sunday as a family. I also attended Church of England primary and secondary schools. Music played a big part in my life. I sang in the cathedral choir and played the clarinet.

As a teenager I got bullied a lot at school, not because I was gay but because I was quiet and very overweight. I was straight-laced, didn't swear and came from a 'nice' family and in a tough school I didn't have a lot in common with the kids around me. They picked on me for being different. I always thought my parents would get divorced just because everyone else's parents were.

When I was younger, homosexuality was never talked about in our house, not through ignorance or arrogance, it just wasn't part of my parents' life. It was only after I came out that I realised my mum's business partner was gay and I had never known. It was never ever mentioned.

When I was 10 or 11 I realised what being gay meant. I was watching a gay character in a television soap, I can't remember which character or which programme but my mum was a fan of *Coronation Street*, *The Bill* and *Casualty* and so it would have been one of those. Then I realised that this other group of people existed. TV opened a window, I heard the word gay used for men who liked men and that name made sense to me. In a household where my parents never really spoke of emotions, it wasn't something that suddenly hit me; it was a slow burner of understanding and slowly realising that it made sense to who I was.

My awakening came during an art class in my first year of high school. I was 12 and had been given an assignment to go through the entire magazine collection in the art room and find a face to draw. I picked an old copy of Attitude magazine with Robbie Williams on the front. As I sat drawing his face, I flicked through the magazine and realised what it was, so I stole it and stashed it away at home. I realised that there were more gay people in the world.

"Looking back I had a childish crush on my best friend in primary school; I just didn't realise it. I was obsessed with him. I wanted to dress like him, I tried to impress him and I always wanted to be around him."

Moving to university in Lancaster did me a lot of good. When I first started university I was shy and introverted partly because of my weight problem and my religious upbringing, but being around different people helped to kick my insecurities out of the door. I came out to my friends in the first year but I wasn't emotionally mature enough to do anything about it. At 19 I weighed 20 stone, so I was very insecure and had issues with my confidence. I was happy that I had told people I was gay. That was good enough for me.

When I was 20 I lost 10 stone. It was weird. I had been overweight my entire life, it was one of the main reasons I got bullied. I had struggled and tried to lose weight but didn't have the determination. My parents would always say we should go on a diet but it was not the motivation I needed. One night I had been out with friends in a nightclub and someone turned to me and made a nasty comment about my size. It made me think about my weight. The following morning I woke up and it was like someone had turned a switch on. I made a conscious decision to lose weight. Within a month I lost three stone, then over the remainder of the year I lost another seven stone. Losing the weight gave me confidence to go out on dates.

During my time at university, the thing that most scared me was telling my parents I was gay. My parents are very important to me and I worried that I would lose them or their love. But I reached a point in my final year where it was killing me not to tell them as everyone else around me, including my twin brother, knew. So in my final year I decided I was going to tell my parents. In my head coming out was going to be an awful lot worse than it actually was. I was too nervous to tell them in person so I sat down and wrote them a letter. I now regret telling them that way, because it was much worse waiting for their response. When I didn't hear from them after a couple of days I felt awful. I wondered if they had received my letter and were ignoring me – or whether the post had been delayed.

As soon as they received the letter they drove up to see me at university and we spent the day together. There were lots of tears but mostly they were upset that I didn't have the belief and trust in them to tell them face-to-face. If I had just had the courage to talk to them it would have saved them from being so upset. My mum wanted to know if I had a boyfriend and I told her no. At the time I wasn't seeing anyone, it may have been easier if I had had a boyfriend, to share the pressure. Then she said, 'So what do you really want to be now?' which might sound odd but she thought that because I had hidden the truth about my sexuality the rest was a lie. In that moment of emotion my mum just thought I must have some secret plan, when the reality was I had no idea what I wanted to be. After I came out I gave Mum and Dad space and time to come around to the news and eventually they were fine.

From that day on, we never really talked about the fact I was gay, it was one of those unspoken things. When I moved to London after winning The Great British Bake-Off in 2010, my mum came down to help me and my twin brother move into our new apartment. I had already been living in London for a while, kipping on a friend's sofa, and I had started seeing my boyfriend Matt. While we were shopping for furniture in IKEA, Mum asked, 'Are you seeing anyone?' For me that was quite a big deal and at first I was shy so I showed her a photo. 'He's cute,' she said, which was what I wanted to hear.

Eight months passed before I introduced Mum and Dad to Matt. Regardless of whether I was straight or gay I would not have wanted to introduce my parents to a partner if the relationship had not been serious. Now he's truly accepted as part of the family. My parents send him birthday cards and Christmas presents and even my grandma asks about him.

I met Matt in 2010 as I was starting to write my first book The Boy Who Bakes. We met via Twitter, which seemed slightly weird at the time. Matt works for the BBC in their drama social media department for programmes like Doctor Who, but he had never watched The Great British Bake Off. One weekend Matt and his sister were visiting their aunt who was a big fan of the show. She told him there was a nice guy on the show and made him watch it under protest. 'He's cute, you should date him,' his sister said about me. So he followed me on Twitter and Tweeted me but I never took any notice.

Before moving to north London, I Tweeted asking for recommendations for places to eat and places to go in the area. Matt replied and we got chatting. We arranged to go out for Sunday lunch in a childish 'Do you want to go for dinner?' way. It was very sweet. For our first official date we met for lunch and spent nine hours in the pub as we had lots to talk about.

Matt became quite involved with the book. We naturally work well together. He has as a good eye for design and I bounced ideas off him. We had been going out for six weeks when I made him a raspberry ripple cake for his birthday. It went down so well I decided to put the recipe in the book. The art director had an idea that at the start of each chapter we should have a photograph showing people in situations where they are eating cake but you can't see their faces. For instance there's a photo of my editor holding a cup of tea and me holding a plate of Nanaimo bars in the Bars and Cookies section. For the cake opening section there's a photo of me and Matt holding hands and a plate of red velvet cake. It took 45 minutes to take the shot and it's the most awkward way of holding hands. But I like the fact it's in there and you can't really tell it's two men holding hands.

When I was chosen to take part in The Great British Bake Off, I prepared myself for what might happen if the media decided to make my sexuality an issue. But it never happened. While we were filming the series, I did have a weird situation. Halfway through the competition each contestant had to go to a hotel room with the producers to find out how they were coping with the stresses of the Bake Off. The producers spent 90 minutes trying to discuss how being gay affected my baking. I was slightly confused and spoke with the executive producer – I'm thankful no part of that filming was used.

Right at the start of my career I made a conscious decision that I would be as open as I am in my private life: after all, Mary Berry gets asked about her family and private life, so why not me? That openness has led to confidence which has helped me a lot. I never had bad press. I have had nasty things written online, but who hasn't? Some people can be idiots online but I take none of that to heart. I'm not presenting a front when I'm on TV, I'm being who I am and that makes me much more relatable. Maybe some TV producers are wary of commissioning things with me on my own, but I've done lots of TV and I have never had anyone say anything negative to me. If someone doesn't want to work with me because I'm gay then I don't want to work with them. But mostly I've had good press because of it. I've been featured in Attitude and *Gay Times* magazines and I'm now writing a column for a gay men's magazine. I was even named one of the world's 500 influential gay men in a magazine, which is ridiculous, but to my 11-year-old self that would have been unthinkable.

"My relationship with my parents is also much closer and honest. It wasn't bad before, but there was always a distance, because I never felt like I was being completely honest by holding part of myself back."

Ultimately it has led to more respect from both sides. Being open is always a good thing.

When I was at secondary school I went through the worst years of my life because of bullying but my advice to other young people is 'give it a few years and life will change for the better'. Maybe it's because it gives you a thicker skin and makes you more determined, but a lot of people I know who were bullied are now successful.

Sue Northover

Entertainer
Born: Kettering, 1974

Best known as:

Rogue Drag King, the only live singing Drag King in Gran
Canaria. Performing at clubs, bars and Pride events all over
Europe. She lives with her wife in Barcelona, Spain

Sue Northover

I have always known I was a gay and attracted to women. Even when I was at infant and junior school I knew I was attracted to girls more than boys. It was a physical and mental understanding of myself without knowing it had a name. When I was growing up, the term 'gay' was not a phrase commonly used, so I didn't recognise that I was gay, just very different from everybody else around me, as I knew no other lesbians or gay men until later in my teenage years.

> **"My teen years were very hard due to my sexuality. Having no one to talk to about my feelings, I felt very lonely."**

I liked the choices, opportunities, characteristics and style of clothes that boys had, but I was physically attracted to girls. At school I was ridiculed if I was ever honest about my feelings for women and there was a constant pressure to find a boyfriend. I didn't even know there were other people like me and I felt very alone. Fortunately my parents had always taught me to be a very confident and strong-willed person, which certainly helped me to survive later on.

Throughout school I was bullied for being different because of the way I dressed and who I loved. One Valentine's Day I was given a card by a friend and the school bully stole it from my bag and read it out loud to other students. I confronted her, telling her she was a very sad person for doing such a nasty thing. It was a risk as she was well-known for hitting other students. I told her 'You can hit me but it won't change what I am.' I must have shocked her as she didn't hit me.

Another time I was taunted in front of my year and other teachers in a spoof awards ceremony about me 'loving' my teachers. The whole ceremony was being filmed so I laughed it off to give the impression it had not upset me.

To survive at school I often turned to academic achievements and, if all else failed, I played the class clown. My love for girls and women was often questioned and called a 'crush' or a 'phase' I was going through. I remember my first crush was on a female teacher at school who was an inspiration and extremely supportive. But generally I felt completely alone and at one stage I even tried taking my own life.

I am not saying that each action and comment the school bullies made about my sexuality did not hurt, it did. But I knew the bullies were wrong to make me feel that way and needed to be stood up to. To counteract the bullying I would never deny who I was. It was always important to me that bullying was stopped in its tracks. As I was strong and could stand up for myself I often intervened to stop bullies from hurting younger students too.

"The first time I came out was when my mum walked into my sister's bedroom where I was and openly asked me if I was gay."

She had always been suspicious of how different I was from my sister and the other girls at school and in our neighbourhood; she would hear me talking about my favourite teacher and other girls I had been very close to at school and, being very astute, she clearly thought it was time to ask me outright. It was an awkward moment. My sister was very embarrassed by the question, but I admired my mum for asking me. Despite feeling like I had been put on the spot, importantly I answered, 'yes'. Very calmly, my mum said 'OK', and went back downstairs to the kitchen and proceeded to cook dinner. It was never spoken about again.

The most frightening aspect of coming out was actually realising what I was and that my feelings had a name. Admitting those feelings and living with the consequences of doing so was pretty scary too.

The best thing about coming out was that I could finally be myself, feel complete and be proud of who I was. I could finally hand on heart say I had nothing to be ashamed of about being me and loving and being attracted to women.

Before I knew I was gay there were key people I admired without me realising why they were an inspiration to me. These included Tim Curry as Frank'N'Furter from the Rocky Horror Show, Lily Savage, Dame Edna, Hinge and Bracket, Larry Grayson, Kenneth Williams, Oscar Wilde and Morrissey. I was attracted to anyone dressing out of the stereotypes created in society. I was drawn to people with strength and determination. At the time there were more openly gay male figures, so the women that inspired me were strong, empowered women, such as teachers at school, female authors and poets like Jane Austen, actresses such as Emma Thompson, Jodie Foster, Sigourney Weaver and Julie Andrews, singers such as Annie Lennox, Joan Jett, Suzi Quatro, Madonna and k.d. lang, comedians Victoria Wood and Julie Walters and sports women such as Virginia Wade, Martina Navratilova, Fatima Whitbread and Steffi Graf. Later when Madonna started dressing in a suit and a top hat I found her equally as attractive. I still like the power of suggestion and I love to challenge any stereotypes, which is why my act now is very male-orientated but has elements of androgyny to keep the audience guessing. Many years later, while on holiday in Brisbane, Australia, I saw a Drag King – a woman dressed up and impersonating a man – perform. I knew that it was a job I would love to do because it incorporated all of my passions in life in one role. I had always wanted to personify the strong male character whilst keeping my femininity. At school I had been into art and performing arts and I had been the singer and songwriter in a local band called Leuba, so I knew it was something I could do. When I returned home to Leicester I saw entered a Drag King competition in my local pub. Dressed up as Captain Jack Sparrow, I sang Suspicious Minds and Great Balls of Fire and won. With that success I created my stage persona Rogue. The one thing I was certain was that Rogue would sing live – not just mime to tracks. I worked on creating a wardrobe of costumes based on great rock stars like Freddie Mercury, Bono, Robbie Williams and John Bon Jovi. And after years of planning, at the age of 38, I launched Rogue on to the gay scene in the UK and when my wife and I moved to Spain 'Rogue' really took off.

Transforming from Sue into Rogue has taken time to perfect. It takes me an hour to get ready for a show. I start by washing and conditioning my thick hair to make it soft, then use the strongest hair gel and hairspray imaginable to flatten it back. I apply my make-up, using foundation followed by black eyeshadow which I use to accentuate the male traits on my face and give myself prominent cheek bones, darkened eyebrows and eyes. I use a black base body paint/facial hair to create my stubble and six o'clock shadow using a sponge and layers of paint. The next stage is to bind my breasts with duck tape. By taping my breasts to the side I give the appearance that I have a male chest. My wife helps me to do this as the tightness has to be exact to allow my lungs room as I sing live. It is essential to get this right as Drag Kings have been known to faint from chest-binding. I then glue fake chest hair to my chest and create shading on my chest. All my costumes are tailored to ensure that the female figure is less accentuated. I wear a pair of tailored underwear that incorporates my codpiece which gives

Rogue a well-endowed package – as drag is all about being larger than life! A lot of my costumes are made of leather, PVC and rubber, so keeping my heat down is essential and I drink a lot of water prior to performance and eat very little on the day.

When I first announced to my family and friends that I was going to be a Drag King it was no less awkward than when I came out as a teenager. As if growing up as a woman who is a lesbian wasn't hard enough, I had now chosen a career that was challenging the whole status quo. Although men in drag are an acceptable form of entertainment, women dressed up as men have a way to go, even though the Victorian music halls were full of women impersonating men and the first recorded drag act was a woman. Apart from some very key close friends and my wife, there was little support for my decision, but like, coming out as gay, I knew this was all down to lack of education and understanding. Over time the support from friends and fans has been overwhelming, though more education is needed both in the straight and gay communities regarding Drag Kings. The main misconceptions are that all Drag Kings are lesbians who wear men's clothing because they want to be men. Statistically a lot are lesbians, but it's not always the case. Another popular misconception is that Drag Kings don't work as hard as Drag Queens or that they are in some way challenging Drag Queens. However I feel that Drag Kings work alongside Drag Queens and the preparation for their performance is just as rigorous as any other drag act. Being a Drag King is a performance and we are still very proud to be women and embrace the power of our male performance with the power of being a woman. The clothing and make-up is just a costume.

My advice to anyone struggling to come to terms with their sexuality would be, 'Don't let anyone tell you who you are and who to love.' Be proud of who you are and stay strong as although your journey is your own, there are people who are there for you and understand what you are going through. There are LGBT groups and helplines, there are gay and lesbian cafes, bars and clubs you can go to and there is a lot of literature and Internet groups you can find more information and help. It does get better, so do not give up hope as there is nothing wrong with who you are and who you love and you are not on your own.

Gareth Thomas

Rugby Union Player
Born: Bridgend, South
Wales, 1974

Best known as:
Former captain of the Welsh
rugby team. Nicknamed
'Alfie' he is the third most
capped Welsh rugby union
player and the first player
to play for his country
100 times. Led Wales to
their Six Nations victory in
2005, the first Grand Slam
victory in 27 years. The first
professional rugby player to
come out.

Gareth Thomas

I had my first sexual encounter with a guy when I was 17. I hated myself so much afterwards I remember trying to scrub myself clean. For me I could not admit to myself I was gay.

"I was the same as most gay teenagers of my generation. I kept my sexuality hidden. I was fearful of the reaction of people around me and rugby was the way of hiding it."

I joined Pencoed Rugby Club when I was 14. I didn't dare speak to anyone of the confusion I was going through. I would join in the homophobic changing-room banter with the rest of my team. We used to share our shower room with the football boys and would call them 'gay'.

After my first encounter I started to lie to my team-mates about what I was up to when we weren't together. I built up a lot of anger because I didn't like who I was when I stepped off the field. I used to relish the chance of being able to hurt someone in a legal way and under the laws of the game I was able to do that. There have been games when I was uncontrollable. If I did not have the rugby field to let out my aggression I'm sure I would have been locked up a long time ago. By hurting people and being aggressive I could be seen to be a tough guy and being tough meant I was not gay.

Throughout my 20s I was lying, trying to make myself straight, I became a master of playing the straight man and I was living in fear of being found out.

At the age of 27 I married Jemma, a girl I had dated on

and off since I was a teenager. I was under the delusion that by forcing myself to be straight I could rid myself of the gay feelings. By getting married in a church, believing in God and believing in my wedding vows, I thought that would be enough and that somehow I could magically make myself normal. I tried hard but I couldn't fight it. The faster I would run the quicker the poison would catch me and engulf me and I would have to get rid of it somehow and for me that was by seeing a guy. I didn't have a 'phase' with men, I just fulfilled my need to rid myself of those feelings for a while. I never cared for the men like I cared for Jemma. At home, Jemma and I were trying for a family, but sadly she kept miscarrying.

The constant lying made me hate myself. When I couldn't handle being around people I would walk alone along the cliffs near my home. During my lowest point I considered killing myself. I hated being Gareth Thomas. I planned to fold my jumper into a pile, like Reginald Perrin, and jump off the edge; but in my mind I could see my mother and father crying and the thought of them being upset was the only thing that stopped me.

After five years of marriage, the pressure was growing and I felt Jemma deserved some honesty. I decided to tell her I was gay and that was the start of the end of our marriage. We tried to make it work, but as time went on we decided to go our separate ways. A few family and friends knew the real reason why Jemma moved out but I still had the burden of keeping the secret from my team-mates.

I carried on playing rugby, I was captain of the Welsh team, but couldn't sleep because of the stress. Around that time Wales were playing Australia before a capacity crowd. I played the worst game of rugby in my life. I was thinking about what was going to happen after the match and not concentrating on the game ahead of me.

When I came off the pitch after that match I looked at myself in the mirror, I didn't recognise who was before me. I sat in the corner of the changing room, which was my routine, and felt really down. I had played badly and let everyone down. Scott, the coach from the opposing team, came into the changing room and spoke to all the players one by one. He had been our coach before and was really close to the team. I was sitting back in my corner as he approached. He just looked at me and asked 'Alfie, what's wrong?' I burst into tears and told him Jemma had left me. He could figure out why. He took me away into the warm-up area, away from the other boys in the team, and said, 'You need to talk about this and you need some help.' He went and spoke to Martyn Williams and Stephen Jones, two players who the whole team looked up to, and asked them if they would meet me for a drink. I had a nervous two hours as I waited at the team hotel until I knew how they would react. When I told them, they were both shocked at first. But Martyn said, 'You are still Alfie. You're still a great player and still my mate.' It was almost a mixture of relief and happiness. The fact I was accepted by my team made it easier.

All my team knew yet still I was not out in public. For the next three years my sexuality was an open secret in Wales.

"As rumours spread my niece started to get bullied at school. I only found out later that the other kids were taunting her with words 'Alfie sucks cock' and 'Alfie's a gay bender.' It affected her to the point where she didn't want to go to school."

In December 2009 I decided to come out in a tabloid newspaper. After 20 years I could stop lying and everyone around me could stop pretending and my niece stopped getting bullied.

Coming out brought me closer to my parents. My mother said she had never suspected anything because I was a macho man. For all the years I had been afraid to tell them because I didn't know how they would react. I had beaten myself up because I was lying to them but when they found out they said they understood why I was 'hiding' not 'lying'. It's hard to admit that I wasted twenty years of my life hiding who I was. I'm passionate that people should be open about their sexuality as soon as they are comfortable with it.

I wish there had been Diversity Role Models workshops when I was in school, where gay men and lesbians stood up and talked about homophobia. It might have saved me years of anguish. But I hope the fact I have shared my experiences will help others. People respect honesty and if you can be honest about who you are, people will respect that too.

Interview adapted from *Gareth Thomas: Coming Out My Secret Past*: A Dragonfly Film and Television/GroupM Entertainment production for Channel 5

Robin Windsor

Professional Dancer
Born: Ipswich, 1979

Best known as:
Professional dancer on *Strictly Come Dancing*, who has partnered Lisa Riley, Patsy Kensit, Anita Dobson and Deborah Meaden. Also toured in the show Burn the Floor.

Robin Windsor

J oining *Strictly Come Dancing* I found myself being cautious about my sexuality for the first time since I was a teenager. I have never been ashamed of my sexuality and campness, but felt I had to tone it down. I was worried about my parents reading something in the press.

"The rest of my family knew I was gay but, as unusual as it may seem, I hadn't actually told my own parents. It's one of those British things, we have never talked about it."

They were waiting for me to bring it up and I was waiting for them. So it was never mentioned. But I didn't want them to have to hear things through other people and being on TV every week in front of 11 million viewers it would have been easy for that to happen.

People assume that if you're a ballroom dancer you must be gay. But that's not really the case. There are a lot of male ballroom dancers who are in relationships with their female partners. During my first season on Strictly in 2010 I was partnered with actress Patsy Kensit. From my understanding she wanted to dance with a gay guy as she didn't want the press to speculate on marriage number five and all that kind of stuff. When I first had my interview with producers they couldn't actually ask me directly if I was gay so they did it in a roundabout way. At the time I was very coy; I tried to keep it to myself but some of my camp mannerisms just popped out. They assumed, and they assumed accurately, that I would make Patsy Kensit very comfortable. Patsy and I became very close and we remained friends after the show.

The following year I was partnered with Anita Dobson, who was just a dream. And this year I have just met my latest partner, Deborah Meaden from *Dragons' Den*

The fact I'm gay is never brought up on Strictly; I just get called camp because I am very camp. With my shaved head and beard, I might look like the sort of person who would beat you up in a dark alley, but inside I'm soft like a teddy bear. If someone doesn't know me they can be quite intimidated – until I start talking they find it quite odd my character is nothing like the way I look. I am probably the butchest-looking person on Strictly.

I was born into a dancing family: my father taught beginner's ballroom dancing and social dancing classes in our hometown of Ipswich. He met my mum when she turned up at one of his classes many years ago. I first fell in love with dancing at the age of three when my parents took me to a class. After that I was hooked on dancing. I would stand in front of a mirror and wiggle my hips at any opportunity.

Throughout my school years I attended dance lessons and took part in ballroom dancing competitions all over the country. While all the boys were playing football after school, I would be at the dance studio rehearsing and going over the steps I had learnt. I won my first competition when I was seven and from that day I knew I wanted dancing to be my future. *Come Dancing* was my absolute favourite programme on TV. I could not miss one episode. It was very cheesy and tacky but it was everything I loved and to me it was the best show on TV. I know of dancers who had so much stick at school for being different, but I never experienced any name-calling. I was a very lucky boy as my school friends and teachers were all behind me and supportive of my dancing. The fact I would go to school with an orange face and a fake tan didn't matter, my entire school were behind me; they made my life really easy.

Most of my school peers assumed I was going to be gay because I was a dancer and all my friends were girls. It was just an assumption that people made. I knew I was gay from about the age of 10 or 11 when I was at high school. I just knew I liked boys and I didn't like girls. I never had girlfriends. I tried to experiment a couple of times but it wasn't right for me. I just knew that I was different. My family always taught me that to be different doesn't mean it's wrong. So I carried on with my life and never let it bother me.

When I was 17 I went to Holland to represent Britain in the Dutch Open. There were six couples from the UK taking part and we all stayed together in a complex. In between the competition there was a lot of drinking and alcohol involved, as you can imagine with large groups of teenagers being away from home. One evening some of the guys in the group decided to play a game of truth or dare. When it was my turn they asked if I had ever had a girlfriend. At first I didn't answer. All the guys in the group suspected I was gay but they wanted to hear it from me. They kept pushing, asking me if I liked girls. Did I have a current girlfriend? They pushed and pushed until I cracked and admitted I was gay.

After coming out I felt awful. I left my friends and told them I was going to bed. I wanted to be alone. I thought what they had just done was the worst thing in history. I stood outside, alone, in the cold feeling rotten. Then one of the boys in our group came out and gave me his jacket to keep warm and I found myself confiding in him. It was done. I had come out and as we talked it felt like a weight had been lifted off me. At first my dance partner didn't believe it was true. And when I told her parents they insisted it was a phase I was going through. I said, 'No. This is who I am and who I'm going to be for the rest of my life,' and in time they came to understand. But I didn't tell my parents.

I had my first serious relationship with a guy named Antonio when I moved to London to train as a professional dancer. It was all a learning curve as I had never had a boyfriend or girlfriend before. But it was a good experience and we still remain friends today.

While training as a dancer I looked up to Jason Gilkison and his dance partner Peta Roby. They were undefeated Latin champions for 18 years from 1981 to 1999 and they were World, British and International Champions. I later got my dream job working with them when I joined the cast of the international hit show Burn the Floor, which they choreographed. For nine years I was on tour with the show, travelling all over the world and living out of a suitcase, and eventually I started to think that I wanted to come home. My friend Natalie Lowe had just left the Burn The Floor for a job as one of the professionals on the BBC's *Strictly Come Dancing*. One day, while I was on tour in Korea, I emailed from my hotel room and said, 'I want to come home.' She put me in touch with the programme producers and after meeting with them they offered me the job on Strictly.

My most successful season on Strictly came in 2012 when I was paired with former Emmerdale actress Lisa Riley, who is the campest woman in the world. She was the biggest personality of the series. We all judged her from the very beginning including me. Everyone was expecting her to be a joke, like the next Ann Widdecombe or John Sergeant. But once we got into rehearsal and we did our Cha-Cha during week one it brought the house down. She was camp, she was fun, and she loved her musical theatre. We were both very similar and just bounced off each other. She became the people's champion and made it to the top five.

During my time on Strictly I have been lucky to have

camp, wonderful, lovely, amazing women to dance with. I could have had partners who didn't necessarily match my personality but the partners I have had so far have fitted me.

One day I would love to see a same-sex couple on *Strictly Come Dancing* but I don't think it is very practical and I know I will upset some people by saying that. A dance like the Argentinean Tango or Paso Doble could be done as a challenge between two guys but ballroom dances just don't work with people of the same sex. When I took part in competitions when I was younger there would be all-girl categories because there were not enough boys to go around – so you could argue that if they can do it in dancing competitions around the world it could be done on Strictly? If it ever did happen my dream partner would be Alan Carr but I'm sure if he ever did the show he would be teamed up with one of the girls.

"Since coming out I have found everyone has treated me exactly the same as they had before, which is how it should be. There was nothing different; I was me all along."

Being in the public eye through Strictly has allowed my personality to come out. I have since posed for the cover of *Gay Times* and for the first time I talked about my relationship with my partner Davide Cini, who I met two years ago on a dating website, which a lot of people laugh about. A lot of people have since thanked me for that for giving then courage and inspiration to do the same.

My advice to younger people is always believe in yourself, and whatever you feel about who you are, and whatever your body is telling you, is always the right thing. You know you're gay from a certain age. I kept it to myself for a long time but you have to accept it yourself before you can tell anyone else. And when you accept it that's when the time is right to tell other people.

In the summer of 2013 I finally came out to my parents. My partner Davide and I were on holiday in New York with Lisa Riley. We were flying in a helicopter over the Statue of Liberty, when I popped the question to Davide. It was all very romantic and he said yes. When we got back to our hotel later that day, I sent my mum an email. It said, 'It might be a lot to take in, but I've just got engaged.' Her reply was, 'That's absolutely wonderful.' When we got back home to London, there was a lovely engagement card waiting for us. It was much easier than I expected it to be – and now everyone's happy. All I have to do is set a date for the wedding.

QBOY
aka
Marcos Brito

Musician
Born: Basildon,
Essex, 1978

Best known as:
UK's first openly gay hip
hop artist and presenter of
Channel 4's '*Coming Out
To Class*'.

QBOY aka Marcos Brito

Q ueer boy. Gay boy. The kids would spit and shout these names at me. I was just nine years old and it was the first time I had ever heard the words queer or gay. It was the label that was applied to me by the school bullies.

I have always been gay. I never turned gay, never thought I was gay and never came out. Everyone just knew. At school I was bullied for not being typically straight. When I was six years old I remember sitting in a field with the girls making daisy chains, rather than playing football with the boys. Automatically I was ostracised for being different. I wasn't posh by any means but I was well spoken and had great communication skills, so I stood out from the average Basildon kid. It made me different and it was another reason to bully me.

My home life was not particularly happy or stable. My father came from La Gomera in the Canary Islands and my mother suffered from bipolar, which was only diagnosed nine years ago, so for most of my childhood she was quite aggressive. My parents spent my childhood fighting and, as my sister was seven years younger, I would always end up as the referee. Through the third and fourth years of junior school the bullying continued and when I got to senior school the problem got worse. When I started my GCSEs, it was a really stressful time.

"At lunch times I would go as far away from school as I could and would sit on my own on a bench in the middle of a housing estate. No one would find me there and I could avoid conflict."

My head of year was also gay, although it was not discussed, and he tried to be as supportive as he could. But he couldn't be there when the kids were hitting and spitting and calling me queer boy. When the stress got too much I would flip out and the consequences would haunt me for a long time afterwards.

One day in class I snapped. A girl, who was the cousin of one of the notorious school bullies, was annoying me by throwing rubbers, pencils and rulers at me from back of the classroom. After the third thing hit my head I flipped out and I don't remember what happened next, but I ended up on top of her, kicking her. The teacher broke us up, but after that I had to make myself scarce to avoid any retaliation from her cousin. It made me hate going to school.

"Every morning I was filled with fear, I didn't know where to go or if I would get caught and beaten. It was so bad that my head of year stepped in and allowed me to leave lessons five minutes early so I could get home safely."

My first love was the pop group Five Star. They taught me how to dance as I copied the steps in their music videos. Then 1989 arrived and the radio stations were full of rap and dance as hip hop met rave culture. I was buzzing off Neneh Cherry, Salt-N-Pepa and Technotronic, who had a female rapper called Ya Kid K. I didn't have many male gay people to look up to but I went crazy for the early American female rappers like MC Lyte and Queen Latifah. Christmas 1991 came and Salt-N-Pepa released their greatest hits album. Every girl in my class and me had the album for Christmas. I would sit together with my girlfriends, listening to it on headphones and singing along. Most of my friends in school were girls but it was very much like the film Mean Girls. One day I would sit with them at lunchtime and everything was OK, the next day I couldn't because I was a boy. On the days the girls did not want to be my friend – I was on my own.

Hip hop was the one thing that connected me with the bullies. The straight boys, who bullied me, were actually the ones who first introduced hip hop into the school. They were into jungle and bands like the rap duo Kris Kross and their taste in music filtered down to me. We wore our clothes backwards and learnt all the raps. I would rap along with the straight boys to Neneh Cherry's 'Buffalo Stance' and 'Manchild'. It made me fit in more with their crew.

I left school at 16 and went to college to study A levels. In the first week I was sitting in the canteen with a girl friend when a group of sporty-type boys walked past and muttered 'queer, gay' under their voices. Right away me and my friend started screaming 'Gay? Who's gay? Who's f***ing queer? We can't have no queers in here.' We went over the top and the boys were so completely embarrassed, they shuffled out of the canteen. We had taken their own words and used them as a weapon against them. My guess is that they had probably never been bullied by a gay person before and didn't do it again. We did this a couple of times and soon no one bullied me again. I never actually came out in college but from day one I became the one bullying the straight boys. I was no longer the victim and I used my confidence about my sexuality to defend myself and make myself bigger.

The first time I immersed myself in gay culture was at the nightclub Heaven. In those days Heaven on a Saturday night was the only place in the UK that was gay and played hip hop and R'n'B. It was only a tiny side room but I could mix with other gay people who were into hip hop.

After graduating from university in contemporary dance, I met DJ Mistermaker, creator of the website gayhiphop. com. For four years I edited the website where I got to interview some of my rap idols and found myself at the centre of 'homo-hop'. From there I picked up the mic and founded the QFam (Queer Family) collective of singers and producers and my DJ crew Pac-Man. I decided to take my rap name QBOY as an abbreviation of the name I was called by the school bullies. The first few gigs were tricky, as gay audiences weren't used to hearing rap music in clubs. They were always polite but did seem rather dazed. I released my first EP 'Even the Women Like Him' in 2004 and a year later I found myself being nominated for Performing Artist Of The Year at the 2005 GALAs, alongside Will Young and Stephen Gately.

Two years later I was asked to present the TV documentary 'Coming Out to Class' for Channel 4. It focussed on my own experiences of bullying and looked at what other teenagers were going through. Although it was six years ago, I still get people messaging me who have just seen it online. People my age really connected with what I had gone through and understood because they went through a similar thing, while younger kids who are in school now also felt the same way.

I'm not a negative person, but if there's one thing I've learnt is that for every shit time you're having it's just a process you need to go through to get somewhere. When you can't see the light at the end of the tunnel you have to realise that the tunnel is taking you somewhere better.

Diana King

Singer/songwriter
Born: Jamaica, 1970

Best known as:
For her chart-topping hits 'Shy Guy' from the soundtrack of
the Will Smith film *Bad Boys* movie and 'Say A Little Prayer'
from the Julia Roberts film *My Best Friend's Wedding*. She
collaborated with Notorious B.I.G. on his track 'Respect' and
Celine Dion on 'Treat Her Like A Lady'. Sold millions of records
worldwide, signed to Madonna's Maverick record label and
now runs her own label ThinkLikeAgirl. Honoured with the
Vanguard Award at the Out Music Awards in Las Vegas in
2012. The first Jamaican artist to ever publicly come out.

Diana King

What made you choose to come out publicly on
Facebook?

The reasons are many but I came out publicly because
I am a public figure who communicates a lot with my fans
on social media, but also it felt like it was my duty to say it
with pride for all those who are like me and afraid. It was
the only thing missing from my life as far as being 100%
authentic was concerned. I have always followed my heart
and said and done whatever it was I wanted to. On 28 June
2012 I had a moment of courage from the fear I had learnt
and I took it. I posted, 'Yes!! I am a lesbian.' My post read
'I am ... woman ... mother ... aunt ... Jamaican ... American
... International artist ... singer ... songwriter ... band leader
... friend ... lover ... entrepreneur ... goddess! among other
things and yes!!!...I am a lesbian ... the answer to my most
asked indirect question. I welcome the 'Who cares' right
now LOL. I answer now, not because it's anyone's business
but because it feels right with my soul ...'

**"I had waited a long time to feel this brave and on that
day I got to the point where I preferred to be hated for
who I am than be loved for an illusion in
people's minds."**

**How did your former husband and son react? How
did people react towards them?**

Love stands the test of time. We are all very close. As for
"people", you can't live your life for others. Your children and
family fall into the category of "others" too. It's better to be

upfront about who you are and how it is, so the right people will love and accept you no matter who they are.

Have there been any negative experiences?

I had a few negative comments but nothing compared to the positive stuff. I must say I didn't expect so much love but it feels great. The only difference now is that I have to think twice about where I go to perform. Even though my fans are everywhere, if it's a country where LGBT people are killed or imprisoned, I won't go. It is frustrating because my music does not discriminate and neither do I. I wish it wasn't like that but I have to be smart and keep my band and me safe.

When and how did you first realise you were gay? You have talked about the negative attitudes towards gay people in Jamaica and the violence levelled at your 'sister-friend.' How did you deal with such levels of homophobia growing up?

I believe I was about five years old when I felt something but the Jamaican culture, which is deeply rooted in Christianity, can turn even an LGBT person homophobic. At the very least, I was quite confused. Initially, I was too young to know what I was feeling and then as I got older I became silent except for when I sang and just tried to fit in because just in case I wasn't "straight" I didn't want to get hurt or murdered. When it started to become more clear to me I knew I had to get away because I did not see myself living in fear or a life where I could not be myself and I knew I could not change the belief system no matter how great I could sing. I didn't just know it, like many people do, it took me into my 20s but I do believe my upbringing made it harder for me to figure out. Who would want to be gay if it means being disowned, or persecuted. If it means oppression or death.

What was the hardest part of having to hide your relationship?

The hardest part of my relationship isn't hiding it. It's knowing that our love is viewed as 'less than' and not accepted, and the rights we are entitled to have to be fought for or proven in courts to be deserved and not just given to us as equal human beings. The hardest part is knowing that being a lesbian can possibly get me or the ones I love hurt or killed.

Has anyone ever advised you to stay in the closet because of your career?

Yes, one person. It was a woman who was on trial to become my manager about eight years ago. She had a big problem with my "JEANZ N T-SHIRT" swag, where I sing 'Simple life, love the simple love, love me Jeanz and me T Shirt, love me sneakers with a little dirt, pin stripe suit and me Converse ... more of me and less of you to myself I've got to be true'. So I had to let her go.

What's been the most memorable/positive experience as a result of coming out?

The most memorable is performing at the Pride Events, I had never done that but the best part is really me being true. Being a lesbian is not all that I am but it was the one thing I always avoided. It is amazing the doors that open when you free yourself from fear. Everything is possible, limitless now.

In what way has being open about your sexuality now helped you as an artist?

It has helped me as a person, which is what I am first.

Coming out has made me more grateful. Grateful for my life, my talent, the love I have for myself and the love that surrounds me and the fans that remain loyal. I believe when you feel complete within yourself and give thanks for all you have in a spiritual way, everything else gets better. Life and everything in it seems more beautiful and everything you do is just more honest. People love drama but they also love when you keep it real.

What advice would you give to any anyone struggling to come to terms with their sexuality?

First, know that you are beautiful and you are not alone. It may be dangerous for you, so find other LGBT people to talk to or write to who understand what you are going through. We are everywhere. Find us and reach out to other LGBT people, people like me.

dianakingdom.com

Darren Scott

Journalist
Born: Scotland, 1978

Best known as:
Editor of *Gay Times*, the UK's leading gay magazine.

Darren Scott

I hold my mother ENTIRELY responsible for the way I turned out! She introduced me to every bloody gay entertainer around. So as a result I grew up loving Boy George, Erasure, Julian Clary, Paul O'Grady, Holly Johnson – every single one.

"It was so early on when I realised I was gay. At junior school I was being bullied for being gay, before I even knew what it was myself."

But looking back I should've known, I was into all the clichés and stereotypes before I even knew what they were, too. So I would say pre-teen, though obviously it was a different time then and you were led to believe that it was in some way 'wrong', so you really didn't say anything.

I was generally happy as a child, very much loved by my family. I'm sure I was a horror of a teenager, though I don't know if keeping the fact that I was gay a secret played into that. I tried to have girlfriends, to fit in, but of course it wasn't really for me.

I think now that I was always out to my friends, though that probably wasn't the case. I certainly left home partly so that I could feel more comfortable being who I really was. That's when I got my first boyfriend and felt I could then come home and tell my mother, who in turn told my grandparents. For some reason I had this bizarre notion in my head that I couldn't come out until my grandparents were dead. This now seems utterly awful to me and I'm so grateful I didn't do that. They loved me so much and said they'd always known, so it wasn't an issue.

Of course in life you're always going to meet arseholes along the way. I believe that being bullied at school helped me develop a thicker skin to these kinds of people and I don't really notice homophobia directed at me personally because I tune it out.

"I had a job once where I was relentlessly victimised by a manager and it wasn't until I left that it was pointed out it was because of my sexuality. I hadn't even considered that. I just thought he was an arsehole. He was, obviously."

He's since lost his job and I'm at parties with my childhood icons!

The best part about coming out is being able to live my life exactly as I want, with no secrecy, no shame, no excuses and not hurting anyone else; it's brilliant. Plus, of course, it's played an instrumental part in what I do for a living.

Gay Times had always been part of my life. I mean, it's been *Gay Times* for 30 years now (having originally started as HIM in 1974). It was the original gay magazine, I've read it ever since I was at college but I could never have considered that one day I might work there, let alone be the editor. I still have 'pinch me' moments'. I originally started working for Pink Paper while I was still at university in Scotland, then moved to London to be features editor on the title. When that sadly closed down in 2008 I moved over to *Gay Times* to become the deputy editor. Now I rock up with my pug Toby every day to edit the magazine, it's something I could never, ever have dreamed of doing when I was a kid. Through my job all those stars that I used to watch on TV with my mum when I was younger, I now get to introduce her to them, which is lovely. In fact, my mother has Andy Bell's signature tattooed on her shoulder. Boy George, Erasure, Julian Clary, Paul O'Grady, Holly Johnson, I still look up to them. They're bloody legends. Meeting Madonna was a highlight of my career, something that teenage gay boy in Scotland from way back when would never, ever have believed. In those days when things were so upsetting and

I looked up to my musical heroes for inspiration to get me through, who would have thought I would grow up and get to share a drink with them.

Going on the Doctor Who Tardis set was also the most incredible thing for a geek like me.

Obviously *Gay Times* has evolved from its original, pre-internet days and the agenda and audience is really quite different. I think now it features gay and straight people who enjoy all aspects of modern-day gay living. I feel that *Gay Times* doesn't tell you that you should aspire to be like anyone else, or to be a certain 'type' of gay man, I hope that our editorial shows us to be as fun and flawed as anyone else – and that that's most definitely an OK place to be.

Through my job I've laughed and cried. I get to hear so many real life stories that actually break your heart, just when you think it was made of stone. And then the comments start to trickle in from readers saying 'thank you' for featuring these things, and how it's helped them. It's quite humbling and really makes you remember that it's such a huge publication.

My advice for anyone struggling to come to terms with their sexuality is 'Relax and enjoy it.' As Belinda Carlisle says 'live your life, be free'.

Sophie Ward

Actress
Born: London, 1964

Best known as:
Star of many stage, film and TV
roles including the hit TV series
Hustle, *Land Girls*, *Holby City*,
Dinotopia and *Law & Order UK* and
Steven Spielberg's *Young Sherlock*.

Sophie Ward

Describe your childhood and adolescence?

I had a very happy, quite eccentric childhood. We were a peripatetic family and I had lots of adventures around the world with my middle sister (I was eleven when my youngest sister was born).

When you were younger were there any LGBT role models you looked up to?

There weren't many famous out lesbians and the representation of lesbians in the media was very negative.

When and how did you realise you might be gay?

I did not know I was a lesbian until I was in my late twenties. It was a slow dawning.

How did you and Rena meet?

Rena and I met in Los Angeles. We knew each other for about a year before we went out. Within a few weeks, my feelings were very strong. I would say, 'love at first kiss!'

Did your role in A Village Affair have any influence on your life choices?

Filming A Village Affair did not really influence my decision but it was a very intense film to make when it reflected my own life so clearly.

In what way has being open about your sexuality

helped you in your career?

Being out to myself has made me feel more grounded and I think it has helped me in many aspects of my life.

What advice would you give to any young people struggling to come to terms with their sexuality?

Take the time to talk to those you love and who love you.

Do you have any advice to other parents on coming out to their children?

They'll teach you loads. Keep listening.

in partnership with ✗✗RBS

About Diversity Role Models ("DRM")

LGBT students are three times more likely to attempt suicide. Seven out of ten lesbian and gay young people say homophobic bullying affects their school work and many have skipped school because of it. One in six has been subjected to death threats, and 52% have heard homophobic comments from teachers and school staff. Since its formal launch in the House of Commons in November 2011, DRM has become one of the UK's most important anti-bullying charities. DRM has already delivered over 265 pro-diversity workshops to over 5,000 pupils using 74 trained role models, communicating directly with students of all ages, using positive role models to counter negative stereotypes based on sexuality. Of these 5,000 pupils, 92% indicated that they would treat a Lesbian, Gay, Bisexual or Transgender (LGBT) person better after the workshop, while 90% indicated that they would use the word 'gay' as a derogatory term less in the future. In addition, after the workshops, only 1% said they would stop being friends with someone who told them they were LGBT, compared to 15% before the workshops started.

www.diversityrolemodels.org